Introducing Hebrews

Charles Ozanne

ISBN: 978-1-78364-493-3

Open Bible Trust

www.obt.org.uk

Open Bible Trust
Fordland Mount, Upper Basildon,
Reading, RG8 8LU, UK.

Introducing Hebrews

Contents

Introduction

The Epistle to the Hebrews has always been of special interest to students of the Bible and dispensational students in particular. Its individual approach, its Old Testament flavour, its interest in typology are features of particular interest. But most important of all is its emphasis on 'maturity', the need to persevere in patience and faith, and the ever-present danger of backsliding and lapsing into denial of the faith. We would be unwise to imagine that we are too 'mature' to fall into this danger. So, if we are honest, we shall see ourselves mirrored in this epistle, either as one who is going on to perfection or as one whose faith has grown cold. I have chosen this epistle not because I think I know all about it, but because I know that I don't and I am anxious to learn more. With that aim in view I invite you to join me in trying to understand the message of Hebrews.

Authorship

The question of authorship is a vexed one to which there is no certain answer. Most readers of *Search* will probably feel that Paul was the author, and certainly some of the most enlightened expositors, Bullinger and Wordsworth for example, have been of this opinion. But most discerning inquirers from the earliest times, including Luther and Calvin, have been very positive that Paul could not have been the author. F.F. Bruce for example declares, "We may say with certainty that the thought of the epistle is not Paul's, the language is not Paul's, and the technique of Old Testament quotation is not Paul's." And again, "He had a copious vocabulary and was a master of a fine rhetorical style, completely different from Paul's." I myself have been greatly impressed by Dean Alford's penetrating discussion of this problem, as the following remarks will indicate. The first thing to do is to build up an identikit of what our author was like.

He was a second generation believer

The writer of Hebrews associates himself with his readers as someone to whom "this salvation, which was first announced by the Lord, was confirmed to us by those who heard him" (2:3). This is not the way in which Paul speaks of his own salvation. In 1 Corinthians 15:8 he says, "and last of all he (the risen Christ) appeared to me also, as to one abnormally born". And in Galatians 1:12: "I did not receive it (his gospel) from any man, nor was I taught it; rather, I received it by revelation from Jesus Christ."

He was a disciple and companion of Paul

There can be no doubt that our author was thoroughly versed in Paul's vocabulary and phraseology, either from familiarity with his epistles or from close attention to his sermons. No one can read the introductory chapter to *Perfection or Perdition* by Welch and Allen without being impressed by the numerous verbal agreements between Hebrews and Paul's acknowledged epistles. Alford says, "Such a degree of acquaintance with the thoughts and writings of St. Paul could hardly, at such a time, have been the result of mere reading, but must have been derived from *intimate acquaintance*, as a companion and fellow-labourer, with the great Apostle himself."

It is interesting to observe however that even the most ardent defender of Pauline authorship (e.g. William Leonard) cannot avoid bringing in a co-author to explain the marked difference in style. Leonard says, "Without destroying his master's claim to authorship such a secondary agent may have a considerable part in the bestowal of those graces which mark a writing as elegant." And again, "There is no reason why we should exclude the literary cooperation of a secretary in the work of stylistic arrangement, choice of words, cutting and filing of phrases that finally resulted in a Scripture, which is one of the great jewels of sacred literature."

The elegance of Peter's first epistle is probably due to the collaboration of Silvanus (1 Peter 5:12). James, whose Greek is reckoned to be some of the best in the New Testament, may also have employed a skilled amanuensis. But can we imagine an accomplished writer like Paul needing the services of a literary stylist? A secretary, yes (e.g. Tertius, Romans 16:22), but not surely a collaborator such as is here envisaged! If Paul cannot have written the whole thing himself, the probability is that he did not write any of it.

The hypothesis that the *matter* is Paul's, but the *diction* another's is tantamount to saying that "the Epistle to the Hebrews is to be ascribed *two different authors*. This theory is refuted by the Epistle itself, which plainly points to *one person* as its author" (Wordsworth). This applies equally to the translation theory mentioned below.

He was a Hellenistic Jew

Our author was a Hellenistic Jew, a man of Greek language and culture, brought up in Greek habits and thought. The excellence of his Greek, and more especially his constant use of the Greek Septuagint version, are proof of this. He takes his place alongside Stephen who also quotes from the Septuagint in Acts 7. It is often said that Hebrews is addressed to Hebrew Christians in Jerusalem or Palestine. But this is most unlikely since the Greek language and version were not used in Palestine, not anyway by those of strict belief (Acts 22:2), and the Hellenistic Jews had been expelled from Jerusalem after the martyrdom of Stephen (Acts 8:1).

Could it be a translation?

Could, however, the rounded and balanced periods of our epistle be explained on the assumption that Paul's original work was translated into Greek by someone else? This has also been suggested but the authorities are adamant that this is impossible. The epistle simply does not read like a translation, and there are many features which argue against it. As Alford says, the peculiarities of the Septuagint version are not infrequently interwoven into the argument, and made to contribute towards the result: which would be impossible, had the Epistle existed primarily in Hebrew. Besides, the prevalence of alliterations and paronomasiae, and the Greek rhythm, to which so many rhetorical passages owe their form, would of themselves compel us to this conclusion."

We have therefore an original composition by a Hellenistic Jew, a disciple and companion of the great Apostle. He does not reveal his name, but his identity was well known to the first recipients of the letter (13:18, 19, 23).

Those from Italy send you their greetings (13:24)

This statement has been understood in two different ways: either that he was writing from Italy or that he was writing to Italy. But if he were writing from Italy would he not have said. "Those *in* Italy send you greetings"? The preposition "from" suggests that "those from Italy" were ex-patriots from Italy who were living in another place. We are probably thinking of men like Aquila, "who had recently come from Italy with his wife Priscilla because Claudius had ordered all the Jews to leave Rome" (Acts 18:2).

The church in Rome began with the "visitors from Rome" who were present on the day of Pentecost and responded to Peter's appeal (Acts 2:10). Alford says, "Here we have a church, the only one of all those with which St. Paul and his companions were concerned, of which it could be said that the Gospel was confirmed to us by those who heard Him." Hence Italy is an eminently suitable place to be the destination of our epistle.

There is evidence that the recipients of Hebrews had suffered persecution after they had received the light (Hebrews 10:32-34). This may refer to harassment by Claudius in 49 or 50 A.D., while Timothy's imprisonment and release, mentioned in 13:23, may have happened under Nero as a result of his association with Paul. It is likely therefore that Hebrews was written to Jewish Christians in Italy and that greetings are sent from "those from Italy", Jewish Christians expelled from Italy by Claudius and now living in the place of writing. Where that place was is not revealed but probably some place frequented by both Timothy and the author – Ephesus possibly.

Who then was the author?

I have not space to go through all the possible contenders. But there is one who stands out above all the rest, and he is *Apollos*. Everything said about Apollos in Acts 18:24 fits our author exactly. He is described as a Jew, a native of Alexandria who had come to Ephesus, a learned (or eloquent) man, with a thorough knowledge of the Scriptures. In Corinth he was second only to Paul himself (1 Corinthians 3:6 "I planted the seed, Apollos watered it, but God made it grow"). So much was this the case that some people were saying, "I follow Apollos" (1:12).

It was probably to avoid a repetition of this sectarian spirit that he withheld his name from this epistle to Hebrew Christians in Italy, if indeed it was he who wrote it. The last thing he would have wanted would be to encourage another Apollos party in opposition to Paul, who was himself in Rome by this time, albeit in prison. But to those to whom this letter was principally addressed his identity would have been well known.

Seeing however that the writer has deliberately withheld his name, should we not respect his wishes in this regard? This epistle is anonymous and intentionally so, and that is how it should remain. However, rather than placing it with Paul's epistles, it more naturally takes its place alongside the Dispersion epistles that follow. Just as Acts gives the historical background to Paul's epistles, so the epistle to the Hebrews gives the theological background to the epistles that follow, including the book of Revelation with which it has much in common.

Introducing "the Son" Hebrews 1:1-3

In olden times God spoke to the fathers in a variety of ways ("in many parts and in many ways"). He spoke in storm and thunder as well as in the still small voice. He spoke to prophets and priests as well as to shepherds and ploughmen. He also made known His word in many different modes and media, such as law, prophecy, parable, proverb, prayer, psalms, symbols, plagues and play-acting. But now "in the last of the days" He has spoken to us "in Son", or Son-wise. Formerly He spoke "in the prophets"; now, as Westcott puts it, "in one who has this character that He is Son". This is God's final revelation to mankind.

In the last of the days (1:2)

This expression occurs about ten times in the Greek Old Testament, either in the singular or the plural, in translation of the Hebrew *be'aharit ha-yamim*, "In the latter days". In some cases it seems to mean no more than "hereafter, in days to come". But especially in the later references there is a clear pointer to the end-times. In Ezekiel 38:16 it is used of Gog; in Daniel 10:14 with reference to a vision of future events; in Hosea 3:5 of Israel's final repentance; in Micah 4:1 of the establishment of the Temple mount as chief among the mountains. This is also the meaning in 2 Peter 3:3 ("in the last days scoffers will come"). Nearest to Hebrews 1:2 is the similar expression in 1 Peter 1:20:

> He was chosen before the creation of the world, but was revealed in these last times for your sake.

Elsewhere in Hebrews it is presupposed that the end-times had come. See in particular Hebrews 9:26:

> But now he has appeared once for all at the end of the ages to do away with sin by the sacrifice of himself.

The expression used here is found elsewhere only in Matthew (13:39, 40, 49; 24:3; 28:20). With the coming of Christ the end, or winding-up, of the ages began. If the Jews had repented in response to the preaching of Christ and His apostles, the second coming would have followed soon after and the last age of all, the millennium, been inaugurated. This is what we find in all the epistles written during the time covered by Acts.

Heir of all things

Seven things are spoken of the Son in vv. 2 and 3. These vv. take their place beside Colossians 1:15-20, Philippians 2:5-11 and Revelation 1:12-18 as one of the great Christological passages. The first thing said of Him is that He was appointed "heir of all things". According to Psalm 2:8:

> I will make the nations your inheritance, the ends of the earth your possession.

But Christ's inheritance is not limited to the earth; it includes "the world to come" (2:5), and indeed "everything", nothing is excepted (2:8).

He made the world

Or better perhaps: "He appointed the ages". The word *aiones* usually means "ages", as in 9:26 (quoted above) and 11:3 probably. But most commentators think the meaning here is wider; according to Bruce, "the whole created universe of space and time". Christ was certainly instrumental in creating all things (Colossians 1:16), whether or not this verse actually says so.

He is the radiance of God's glory (1:3)

Not simply the reflection (as in the RSV), but the light itself – "the radiance shining forth from the source of light". Light itself is invisible. "The light of the knowledge of the glory of God" is to be seen only "in the face of Christ" (2 Corinthians 4:6).

He is the exact representation of God's being

He is the impress of God's being, the stamp of His nature. The word *character* (from *charasso*, to engrave), is used especially of the impression or stamp on coins and seals. The word translated "being" is *hupostasis*. In other places it means "confidence" (2 Corinthians 9:4; 11:17; Hebrews 3:14; 11:1), but here it has a different meaning – "that which underlies". Christ is the visible manifestation of God's underlying person, as we read in Colossians 1:15, "He is the image of the invisible God."

He sustains all things by His powerful word

According to Bruce, "He upholds the universe, not like Atlas supporting a dead weight on his shoulders, but as One who carries all things forward on their appointed course." Having created the world, He now sustains it, bears it along, by His powerful and authoritative word. If He were to cease to do so, the whole thing would grind to a halt and disintegrate.

He provided purification for sins

The aorist participle indicates the 'once-for-all-ness' of His atonement in contrast with the continuous exercise of His powerful word in sustaining the universe. The Old Testament sacrifices had to be repeated endlessly year after year since those offerings were unable to cleanse once for all (10:1-4).

He sat down at the right hand of the Majesty in heaven.

References to Psalm 110:1 are frequent in the New Testament, ever since our Lord silenced the Pharisees from this passage (Matthew 22:41-46). Later in the epistle the author expands on this theme. Jesus our High Priest, he says, is seated at the right hand of the throne of the Majesty in heaven, a minister of the true sanctuary, set up by the Lord (Hebrews 8:1-2). see also 10:11-12. Day after day the priests would remain standing to perform their religious duties. But when this Priest (Christ) had offered for all time one sacrifice for sins, He sat down at the right hand of God.

Commentaries referred to are by B.F. Westcott and F.F. Bruce, both entitled "The Epistle to the Hebrews".

Superior to the angels
Hebrews 1:4-14

As a result of His once-for-all sacrifice Jesus has become infinitely superior to the angels. This was not always the case since for a little while He was made lower than the angels (2:7). But He who was made lower than the angels is now crowned with glory and honour because of the suffering of death (2:9).

"Better" (or superior, *kreitton*) is a recurring theme in this epistle[1], occurring 13 times (see the *KJV*). We have better things (6:9), a better than Abraham (7:7), a better hope (7:19), a better covenant based on better promises (8:6), better sacrifices (9:23), a better possession (10:34), a better country (11:16), a better resurrection (11:35), something better for us (11:40), and the blood of sprinkling which speaks a better word than the blood of Abel (12:24).

"More excellent" (*diaphoroteros*) occurs in Hebrews 8:6 – of a more excellent ministry. Here, in 1:4, the more excellent name that Christ has inherited is that of "Son" as the next verse explains.

There follow seven quotations, mostly from the psalms, which provide proof of Christ's immeasurable superiority to the angels. It is instructive to see which psalms were considered at that time to speak most clearly of Christ. The whole of each psalm should be read rather than just the verse or verses quoted.

---

[1] For more on the theme of Christ's superiority in Hebrews see the last chapter of this book entitled *More on Hebrews.*

Psalm 2:7 (Hebrews 1:5)

> Thou are my Son, today I have begotten thee.

Our author, as always, quotes from the Septuagint, but in this case the Hebrew is the same. The word "beget" is the same as in Matthew 1 (and Hebrews 11:23) and implies a point in time when the Son was begotten. According to Acts 13:33 this was fulfilled when Jesus was raised from the dead and the same is implied in Romans 1:4. He was however already a Son at His incarnation in Hebrews 5:8 ("Although he was a Son, he learned obedience from what he suffered"), and this is confirmed by the Gospels where He repeatedly accepts the title of Son of God. I conclude therefore that He became Son of God when "God sent the Son into the world" (John 3:17), that He was declared Son of God in power at His resurrection (Romans 1:4), and that He will reach His full potential as Son when He is installed as King on the holy hill of Zion (Psalm 2:6).

2 Samuel 7:14

The last quotation is confirmed by the words of Nathan to David with reference to Solomon:

> I will be his Father, and he will be my Son.

This prophecy was not exhausted in Solomon as the concluding words make clear:

> Your house and your kingdom shall endure for ever before me; your throne shall be established for ever. (7:16)

Neither Solomon's temple nor his kingdom lasted for ever. Both however will be established for ever by David's greater Son.

Deuteronomy 32:43 (Hebrews 1:6)

The Septuagint says:

> Let all the sons of God worship him. Rejoice ye Gentiles, with his people, and let all the angels of God strengthen themselves in him.

The wording is the same except that "sons of God" has been replaced by "angels of God" from the next clause. These words come near the end of the Song of Moses. Here God avenges the blood of His servants, and the nations rejoice with His people. The Song concludes, "and the Lord shall cleanse the land of his people" (Hebrew: "shall make atonement for his land and people").

The only problem is that the words quoted do not appear in the Hebrew text of Deuteronomy. Welch thinks the Septuagint is here correct and that the words have fallen out of the Hebrew text. More probably the author is simply quoting from the Septuagint, as he does throughout the letter. Though the words do not appear in the Hebrew, they are in keeping with what the Hebrew says.

The words "Let all God's angels worship him", are quoted from Deuteronomy 32:43 (the Septuagint). These words are prefixed in Hebrews with the words,

> And again, when God brings his firstborn into the world, he says …

But there are some who would translate with the Revised Version, "And when he again bringeth …" The authorities are divided, but in either case the reference would seem to be to the second coming.

The word *protokos*, firstborn, is one of the weighty words of the New Testament. In Romans 8:29 Christ is called "the firstborn among many brethren"; in Colossians 1:15 "the firstborn of all creation"; in 1:18 "the firstborn from among the dead"; and in Revelation 1:5 "the firstborn from the dead". In all these references it is His resurrection which is in mind.

The most significant Old Testament reference is Psalm 89:27:

> I will also appoint him my firstborn, the most exalted of the kings of the earth

These words are spoken of David but, at the time of writing, David's crown had become defiled in the dust, his strongholds had been reduced to ruins, and he had become the scorn of his neighbours (vv. 38-45). Only in David's greater Son could these promises be fulfilled.

Psalm 104:4 (Hebrews 1:7)

> He makes his angels winds, his servants flames of fire.

The thought seems to be that the angels appear to us in the shape of winds and flames of fire. This is how the Septuagint (and *KJV*) have translated the Hebrew, but most modern versions tend to put it the other way round: "He makes winds his messengers, flames of fire his servants." Either way the angels are quite insignificant as compared with the Son.

Psalm 45:6-7 (Hebrews 1:8-9)

This psalm is quoted in vv. 8 and 9. It celebrates a royal wedding, but the royal bridegroom is addressed in language which would be blasphemous if addressed to a mere man:

Your throne, O God, will last for ever and ever.

The last clause should probably be translated in the same way.

> Therefore, O God, thy God has anointed thee with the oil
> of gladness above thy fellows. (NEB)

While inappropriate with reference to David of any of his successors, these words are quite properly addressed to Israel's Messiah, the Lord Jesus Christ.

Psalm 102:25-27 (Hebrews 1:10-12)

Here also the Son is addressed.

> In the beginning, O Lord, you laid the foundations of the
> earth, and the heavens are the work of your hands. They
> will perish … But you remain the same, and your years will
> never end.

In the Psalm it is the Lord who is addressed, but since it was by means of the Son that God created the world, what is said of the Father applies equally to the Son.

> Thou art the same (*ho autos*) and thy years will never end.

The same is said of Christ in Hebrews 13:8:

> Jesus Christ is the same (*ho autos*), yesterday and today and
> for ever.

Psalm 110:1 (Hebrews 1:13)

We have moved full circle and are now back to the psalm referred to in v. 3 ("he sat down at the right hand of the Majesty on high"). This is the psalm which says:

> You are a priest for ever, in the order of Melchizedek. (v. 4)

And that is the theme of Hebrews 6 and 7.

Do not drift away
Hebrews 2:1-4

For the best part of a chapter the epistle has been telling us how much superior to the angels is the Son of God. The reason for this is made clear in chapter 2:1-4 to which we now turn. Whereas the law was mediated by angels (Galatians 3:19; Acts 7:53), the great salvation which is now in view was announced by the Lord Jesus Himself and confirmed by those who heard Him. It behooves us therefore to pay the closest possible attention to what we have heard, avoiding at all costs the subtle temptation to drift away.

This word "drift away" is explained by Bullinger as "being carried away beside *or* floating away past anything with the stream". The danger envisaged is that of slipping away, flowing with the stream. It can happen so easily but the consequences, the just recompense, could be extremely costly.

How shall we escape? (2:2-3)

To neglect so great a salvation is a very serious matter involving incalculable loss to the perpetrator. The same verb "escape" occurs again in 12:25 in a context similar to this one.

> If they did not escape when they refused him (Moses) who warned them on earth, how much less will we (escape) if we turn away from him (Christ) who warns us from heaven.

Similar warnings are to be found throughout the epistle, 3:7 for example, and most alarmingly of all, 10:28-29:

Anyone who rejected the law of Moses died without mercy on the testimony of two or three witnesses. How much more severely do you think a man deserves to be punished who has trampled the Son of God under foot …?

The pressure to renounce the faith, or quietly to drift back into Judaism, must have been tremendous for those living in Italy in the days of Nero's reign of terror. Even for us, who are under no such pressure, there is a real danger of slipping back into the ways of the world, of returning to our former haunts and habits. The penalty for so doing will become clearer as we proceed.

The recompence of the reward (2:2 *KJV*)

Misthapodosia, payment of wages, is a favourite word of our author. The abstract noun occurs three times and the personal noun once, only in this epistle. It is not only the law which has its just recompence and reward, so does obedience (Hebrews 10:35, 11:26), for He is the rewarder of those who earnestly seek Him (Hebrews 11:6). Even Moses regarded disgrace for the sake of Christ as of greater value than the treasures of Egypt. Why?

> Because he was looking ahead for the recompence of reward (Hebrews 11:26)

How much should we who have the example of Christ Himself?

Salvation (2:3)

The great salvation, of which this epistle speaks, has a future dimension which we do not normally associate with the word. The ministering angels of chapter 1:14 are sent forth to serve "those who are about to inherit salvation". This salvation is clearly future, as it is in 9:28:

He will appear a second time, apart from sin, to them that wait for him, unto salvation.

Here salvation is something which takes effect at the second coming. This also is its sense quite frequently in the Old Testament (e.g. Psalm 14:7; 98:2) as well as the New (e.g. 1 Thessalonians 5:9). Salvation is never just for this life; its completion in the future is never far from mind. Salvation in the conventional sense can never be forfeited but there are future aspects of it which may be lost. These are the better things that belong to salvation in chapter 6:9, but there is no reason for anyone to forfeit them so long as he is diligent to the very end, so making his hope sure (6:11).

Firmness

This is another favourite theme of our author. The message declared by angels was indeed firm, and every violation and disobedience received its just penalty. But the salvation now on offer was even firmer, not only announced by the Lord Himself, but confirmed by those who heard Him. It was moreover borne witness to by signs, wonders, and miraculous gifts of the Holy Spirit, distributed as He willed (2:4). These miraculous gifts "formed the most conclusive demonstration and seal of the truth of the gospel" (Bruce).

Their frequent and ubiquitous occurrence is of course presupposed, as the New Testament in general bears out. Paul also appeals to them as proof that the Christian message had stronger validation than the law (Galatians 3:5).

The firmness of our salvation should be matched by our own firmness and resolve. Let us therefore "hold fast our first confidence firm to the end" (3:14). "Every day" we should encourage one another so that no-one is hardened by the deceitfulness of sin (3:13). And all the more so, seeing that our hope is an anchor of the soul, firm and secure (6:19).

We see Jesus crowned with glory and honour
Hebrews 2:5-18

So far the writer has emphasized the superiority of the Son over the angels. To none of the angels did God ever say, "You are my Son", or "Sit at my right hand until I make your enemies a footstool for your feet." On the contrary: the angels are simply ministering spirits sent to serve those who will inherit salvation. True, the Law of Moses was "a message spoken by angels". But what is the law compared with that so great salvation "first announced by the Lord" and "confirmed to us by those who heard him"?

Crowned with glory and honour (2:5-8)

It is not to angels that God has subjected the world to come but to the Son of Man. This is proved by Psalm 8 which is here quoted. We read here that the "son of man", though "made little lower than the angels", God nevertheless "crowned with glory and honour and put everything under his feet".

In the Hebrew it says, "You made him a little lower than *God*", which the *NIV* somewhat arbitrarily translates "heavenly beings", but the Septuagint (which our author consistently uses) says "angels". Again, the Hebrew speaks of mankind in general whose honourable destiny is to be ruler over the world we live in (flocks and herds, beasts, birds and fishes).

This is man's inheritance as promised in Genesis 1:26. But apart from *the* Son of man, Christ Jesus, no man can inherit anything. Hence in Hebrews this psalm is interpreted of Christ. And it is not simply the earth over which He has been made ruler, but "everything" -in heaven and on earth and under the earth (Philippians 2:10); rule, authority, power, dominion, and every title in existence (Ephesians 1:21).

As yet, however, we do not see everything made subject to Him (v. 8). What we do see is "Jesus…now crowned with glory and honour because he suffered death…for everyone".

Perfect through suffering (2:10)

He himself was made perfect through suffering, and that with a view to "bringing many sons to glory". Likewise in chapter 5:9, 10: "He learned obedience from what he suffered and, once made perfect, he became the source of eternal salvation for all who obey him." By so doing He became the author (pioneer or trailblazer) of their (and our) salvation. It is however only in resurrection that He and we are perfected (11:40; 12:23).

He is not ashamed to call them brothers (2:11-13)

The Lord Jesus is not ashamed to call them brothers, because He and they are "all of one (family)". This point is proved by Psalm 22:22, an explicitly Messianic psalm. Here the suffering Christ says, "I will declare your name to my brothers; in the presence of the congregation (*ekklesia*) I will sing your praises," Proof is also found in Isaiah 8:17-18 where the prophet Isaiah stands for Christ. Here our author finds two proof texts separated by "And again". The first line refers to Christ alone ("I will put my trust in him"); the second to Christ and the children of God ("Here am I, and the children God has given me"). One of these children was Shearjashub, "A Remnant will return", who symbolised the believing remnant in Isaiah's day.

Jesus was not ashamed to call them brothers. That was literally true – Matthew 28:10: "Go and tell my *brothers*…" But it was only after the resurrection that He addressed His disciples as brothers (though see Matthew 12:48, 49; 25:40).

He shared in their humanity (2:14-18)

Since the children have flesh and blood, He too shared in their humanity (lit. "the same things") so that by His death He might destroy him who holds the power of death – that is, the devil. Actually "blood and flesh" (not "flesh and blood" as arbitrarily inverted in most versions), "the vital element, the seat of bodily life, the blood being name first to emphasize that the humanity of our Lord was *vitally* human" (G. H. Lang).

He who holds the power of death is (potentially) destroyed, and consequently the fear of death which holds all men in abject bondage is removed for those who truly believe. That is, in proportion to our faith, death should have no qualms for us.

John Wesley was once asked what he would do if he were told he had only three months to live. The great man opened his diary and read out his engagements! For him there was no fear of death.

He did not *take* (the nature of) angels, but *took* the seed of Abraham (v. 16). He became like His brothers in every way, that He might become a merciful and faithful high priest in matters God-ward.

It was because He suffered, being tested, that He is able to identify with us in our temptations and trials. And it is because He endured to the end without wavering that He is seen to be faithful. It is because He has been through it all Himself that He is able to sympathise with us in our infirmities and "to help those who are being tempted". He is therefore very well qualified to assume the role of "a merciful and faithful high priest", and in that capacity to make atonement for the sins of the people".

That He might make atonement (2:17)

The verb *hilaskomai* means "to propitiate" but not in the sense of making an angry God more favourably inclined (as in pagan religion), but in the sense of removing guilt and the remission of sins. As W.E. Vine says, "Through the propitiatory sacrifice of Christ, he who believes upon Him is by God's own act delivered from justly deserved wrath, and comes under the covenant of grace."

The *KJV* "to make reconciliation for the sins of the people" is unfortunate, since (to quote Vine again), "Never is God said to be reconciled, a fact itself indicative that the enmity exists on man's part alone, and that it is man who needs to be reconciled to God, and not God to man."

The verb occurs again only in Luke 18:13, "God, *have mercy* on me (be propitious to me), a sinner", the words of the tax collector in the parable. The related noun *hilasterion* a place of propitiation or mercy-seat, occurs in Romans 3:25 and Hebrews 9:5.

Do not harden your hearts
Hebrews 3

Those addressed in this epistle are called "holy brothers, sharers of a heavenly calling" (3:1). The word for "heavenly" (*epouraniois*) is the same as in Ephesians where the saints are blessed "in the heavenly (places)". Is therefore the heavenly calling the same in Hebrews as in Ephesians? Most people would answer in the affirmative.

The heavenly calling is defined in 11:16 as "a better country, a heavenly one", and in 12:22 as "Mount Zion … the heavenly Jerusalem, the city of the living God". This is the New Jerusalem on whose gates are written the names of the twelve tribes of Israel and on whose foundations are the names of the twelve apostles of the Lamb (Revelation 21:12-14). This city (which will adorn the new earth) is the future residence of the patriarchs, the Old Testament saints, the twelve apostles, and the saints of the Acts period (Galatians 4:26 "our mother"). But, if we are not completely on the wrong track, it is not the true home or mother of the Church of today.

Christ's session at the right hand of God is stressed in this epistle (1:3, 13; 8:1; 10:12; 12:2 cp. 4:14), and this is "in the heavenly places" according to Ephesians 1:20. But there is no suggestion in Hebrews that there is anybody there with Him or that God's right hand is the destiny of the brethren. Hence the heavenly Jerusalem belongs to the heavenly calling of Israel (an associated Gentiles), but the heavenlies themselves are the present (and future) sphere of blessing for believers today.

Greater than Moses (3:1-6)

In the first two chapters of Hebrews there is emphasis on the place of angels. It is demonstrated from an array of Old Testament texts that Christ is immeasurably superior to the angels. Though made a little lower than the angels "for the suffering of death", that lowliness was reversed at the resurrection when He was "crowned with glory and honour".

The gist of 3:1-6 is that Christ is no less superior to Moses. Just as the builder of the house is worthy of greater honour than the house itself, so "Jesus has been found worthy of greater honour than Moses". Moses was a faithful household servant in God's house (cp. Numbers 12:7). Christ also was faithful, but He was faithful as "a son over God's house".

The house is not a literal house, but the house of Israel, the believing community. We are His house, says v. 6, "if we hold fast to our courage (*parresia*) and the hope of which we boast. The need of *parresia* (confidence, boldness) is emphasised in this epistle (4:16; 10:19, 35), while "boasting in the hope" is virtually the same as in Romans 5:2 – "And we rejoice (boast) in the hope of the glory of God."

"Today, if you hear his voice" (3:7-11)

There are many lessons to be learnt from Israel's experience in the wilderness. Some of these are drawn and applied in 1 Corinthians 10. But here Psalm 95 is quoted with a specific purpose in mind, to point out God's justified anger with that generation and the oath He declared in His anger, "They shall never enter my rest".

The Holy Spirit in Psalm 95 solemnly warns the people:

> Today, if you hear his voice, do not harden your hearts as you did in the rebellion, during the time of testing in the desert, when your fathers tested and tried me and for forty years saw what I did.

The words "rebellion" and "testing" are translations of Meribah and Massah, as found in Psalm 95:8. The particular reference is to their rebellion at Rephidim when they petulantly demanded water from Moses. The place was called Meribah and Massah "because the Israelites quarreled and because they tested the Lord saying, 'Is the Lord among us or not?'" (Exodus 17:1-7). But this was not an isolated case: all through the 40 years "your fathers tested and tried me", provoking the Lord to anger at their disobedience.

The outcome was the Lord's angry oath: "They shall never enter my rest." But what is meant by the Lord's rest? Clearly something more is implied than entering the land of Canaan or achieving rest from all their enemies (Joshua 21:44; 23:1). They took possession of the land under Joshua, but Joshua did not give them rest (4:8), nor even David (4:7), nor anyone since for "there (still) remains a Sabbath-rest for the people of God" (4:9). The attainment of rest is nothing less than the realization of their national destiny, inseparably linked with the coming of Christ.

They had the opportunity of entering this time of rest during the 40 years in the wilderness, but they miserably failed. The question is, would the generation of the Acts period do any better than the generation in the wilderness? The writer says:

> See to it, brothers, that none of you has a sinful, unbelieving heart that turns away from the living God. But encourage

one another daily, as long as it is called Today, so that none of you may be hardened by sin's deceitfulness. (vs. 12, 13)

So long as the door remained open, every day was "Today". But the time was approaching when the door would be closed, and then the opportunity could be lost for many hundreds of years. How desperately important it was that they should encourage one another daily, for so long as it was called "Today".

On whom did it depend?

The writer speaks to believers, "holy brothers, who share in the heavenly calling" (3:1). But surely, it was not their response which mattered (had they not already made their choice?), but the response of the still uncommitted majority? But the Israelites in the wilderness were also a redeemed people. The Lord forgave them for their refusal to enter the land from Kadesh-barnea. Nevertheless the judgment remained firm:

> Not one of them will ever see the land... No-ne who has treated me with contempt will ever see it.
>
> (Numbers 14:20-24)

In the Acts period it was the same. The return of the Lord and the attainment of rest depended as much on those who believed as on those who did not. It was the wavering of believers which was chiefly responsible for the delay in the Lord's return. The "ifs" and warnings of this epistle have to been seen in the light of the national emergency then current.

Verse 12 presents a strange anomaly:

> See to it, brothers, that none of you has a sinful (evil),
> unbelieving heart that turns away (*apostatises*) from the
> living God.

Is it really possible for a brother to have an evil, unbelieving heart
and to be in danger of apostatising from the living God?
Regrettably it is – even we are not immune (1 Corinthians 10:6-
12). But in the case of these Hebrews there were pressures and trials
(both from their fellow Jews and from outside) which presented a
severe trial to their faith. They were under constant pressure to
revert to the comparative safety of Judaism, to soft-pedal if not
renounce their Christian commitment.

A Sabbath-rest for the people of God Hebrews 4:1-13

The comparison between "them" and "us" is continued in chapter 4. The good news of the gospel was preached to *them* (those to whom Moses preached in the wilderness), just as it has now been preached to *us*. But, disappointedly, the message they received did not profit them, because their hearing it was not conjoined with faith. The message they received would include such passages as Exodus 19:3-6 and 23:20-33, where Israel was told of their favoured status in God's sight and their glorious destiny as God's people, but also the faith and obedience expected of them without which the promises would come to nothing.

At this point our author quotes again the words of Psalm 95:2: "So I declared on oath in my anger they shall never enter my rest."

They are a statement of God's judgment in the past, but also a stark reminder of what could so easily happen again if the gospel message was not received with faith and obedience. This quotation is a *non sequitur* if connected with v. 3 ("Now we who have believed enter that rest"). Clearly it follows on from v. 2, bypassing the aside in v. 3.

God rested from all His work (4:3-6)

A new aspect of the promised rest is introduced at the end of v. 3:

And yet his work has been finished since the creation of the world.

This rest is not simply the rest which God has reserved for His people, it is "*my* rest", that is God's very own rest. The rest which He assumed on the seventh day, when "He rested from all the work creating that He had done" (Genesis 2:2). It is implied that God began to rest on the seventh day and has continue to rest ever since. Believers may enter here and now into the enjoyment of this rest, though the rest itself will not be visually realized and experienced until its fulfilment in the future. Hence "it still remains that some will enter that rest" (v. 6).

A Sabbath-rest (4:7-11)

Because it is God's rest which He began on the seventh day of creation it is called a *Sabbatism* in v. 9. This word is translated Sabbath-rest in the *NIV*, though *Sabbath-keeping* would be more correct, since the verb *sabbatizo* means "to keep sabbath" in the Septuagint.

> There remains then a *Sabbath-keeping* for the people of God; for anyone who enters God's rest also rests from his own work, just as God did from his.
>
> (v. 9, 10)

The future bearing of this rest is confirmed by the words just quoted, since there is no rest for the honest labourer so long as his life on earth continues. With this agrees Revelation 14:13. John hears a voice from heaven:

> Write: "Blessed are the dead who die in the Lord from now on." "Yes," says the Spirit, "they will rest from their labour, for their deeds will follow them."

It is therefore in resurrection that the promised time of rest will find its full expression for the believer.

This rest was first offered to the people of Israel at the time of the Conquest under Joshua. The land was conquered, for the most part, but the time of rest was not established. It was again on offer when the Monarchy was set up in the time of David, but once again the people hardened their hearts as in the rebellion. It was again on offer when Christ was on earth urging the people to repent in view of the Kingdom of Heaven which was soon to be inaugurated. This time they crucified their Messiah, trampling the Son of God under foot (Hebrews 10:29). Amazingly it was offered to them again during the book of Acts with the result that, when this epistle was written, there still remained a Sabbath-keeping for the people of God. So when will this elusive time of rest finally be experience?

The Millennium?

Will it be the Millennium? No, says F.F. Bruce: "The identification of the rest of God in the Epistle to the Hebrews with a coming millennium on earth has, indeed, been ably defended; but it involves the importation into this epistle of a concept which in fact is alien to it."

Bruce however admits: "It is evidently an experience which they do not enjoy in their present mortal life, although it belongs to them as a heritage… (it is) the eternal homeland which is the heritage of believers… the 'better country, that is, a heavenly' which they desire, the 'city which God has prepared for them (11:16) …'" "It may be," he says, "that in resurrection they, 'in company with us', are to attain this perfection and enter into God's rest."

This being the case, it is difficult to understand why he objects so strongly to the identification of this rest with the coming millennium when, at the first resurrection, Israel's national (and personal) hopes will be realized in full. It is due in part to the anti-millennium prejudice which has determined the prevailing wind of doctrine since long before the Reformation. For some reason 'reformed' theologians find it impossible to believe that the distinction between Jew and Gentile will ever be reinstated again, in spite of the covenants and promises made to Israel and the hundreds of prophecies which predict their restoration in the last days.

But, specifically, it is the type of interpretation to be found in the apocryphal Epistle of Barnabas that Bruce objects to. This epistle says, "Pay attention, children, to the meaning of the words 'He finished it in six days'. It means that in 6,000 years the Lord will bring everything to completion. For the 'day' with Him is a thousand years…" (15:4). So after 6,000 years will be the Sabbath-rest for one thousand years, after which will be "the eighth day, that is, the beginning of the new world".

This interpretation is particularly tempting at the present time when the first 6,000 years of world history have just concluded, or are about to conclude. But Bruce is doubtless correct that this is a concept which is alien to the Hebrews epistle. This epistle says nothing about the preceding ages, but only that God rested on the seventh day, an eternal rest which one day His people will share with Him in the New Jerusalem or on the New Earth.

The Word of God (4:12-13)

> For the word of God is living and active. Sharper than any double-edged sword, it penetrates even to dividing soul and spirit, joints and marrow; it judges the thoughts and attitudes of the heart. (4:12)

The meaning is that "the word of God probes the inmost recesses of our spiritual being and brings the subconscious motives to light" (Bruce). Indeed:

> Nothing in all creation is hidden from God's sight. Everything is uncovered and laid bare before the eyes of him to whom we must give account. (4:13)

See to it, therefore, that none of you has a sinful, unbelieving heart that turns away from the living God (3:12).

Jesus the Great High Priest Hebrews 4:14-5:14

Only in Hebrews are we told about Jesus in His role as High Priest in the order of Melchizedek. In his epistles Paul never uses the word "priest" at all. We are left in no doubt that "Christ loved us and gave himself up for us as a fragrant offering and sacrifice to God" (Ephesians 5:2). But He is only presented as the sacrificial offering, never as the priestly offerer. In Hebrews, on the other hand the word "priest" is used of Christ six times, and "high priest" ten times. The terminology is Jewish, but what is said about Christ in His capacity as High Priest will be found to apply to us as well.

He is able to sympathise with our weaknesses

Even the Jewish high priest was "able to deal gently with those who are ignorant and are going astray, since he himself is subject to weakness" (5:2). How much more is our Jesus able to sympathise with our weaknesses! He was not only fully human, but was tempted in every way, just as we are – yet without sin. "Let us then approach the throne of grace with confidence, so that we may receive mercy and find grace to help us in our time of need" (4:16). In like manner Paul encourages us to approach God, in Christ and through faith in Christ, with freedom and confidence (Ephesians 3:12).

He is the source of eternal salvation for all who obey Him

"Son though he was" -Son of God not simply a son – "he learned obedience from what he suffered and, once made perfect, he became the source of eternal salvation for all who obey him" (5:8-9). It was not obedience as such that He learnt since there was never a time when He was not obedient. What He learnt was *the price* of obedience. And what a harvest of souls His obedience has accomplished! Through the obedience of this one Man many will be made (and have been made) righteous (Romans 5:19).

Especially in Gethsemane (though doubtless on other occasions) "he offered up prayers and petitions with loud cries and tears to the one who could save him from death, and he was heard because of his reverend submission" (5:7). It was through suffering that "the author of their (and our) salvation" was made perfect (2:10).

Again it was not death itself from which He sought deliverance, since it was for this very reason that He came into the world (John 12:27). It was the *agony and grip* of death against which He prayed. We are told that He was heard for His godly fear, for "God raised him from the dead, freeing him from the agony of death, because it was impossible for death to keep its hold on him" (Acts 2:24).

Christ did not take upon Himself the glory of becoming High Priest

No-one takes this honour upon himself; he must be called by God, just as Aaron was (5:4). Aaron's appointment is described in Exodus 28. Many of his successors were not appointed by God at all. In the time of Christ they were routinely appointed by Herod. For that reason some of the pious Jews refused to recognise them, and rightly so since they lacked the necessary qualification, selection by God.

Christ's selection by God is mentioned in two of the writer's favourite psalms: Psalm 2:7 (already quoted in Hebrews 1:5) "You are my Son; today I have become your father" (or, "begotten you"), and Psalm 110:4 (in 1:13 the first verse was quoted) "You are a priest for ever, in the order of Melchizedek."

The subject of Melchizedek, the exalted "King of Righteousness" to whom Abraham paid a tenth of the plunder taken from the slaughter of the kings, is taken up at length in Hebrews 7. We may think this obscure king of Salem has nothing to do with us, but as already mentioned, the office Christ performs for Jewish Christians in His capacity as High Priest, He performs for us as Head of the body, our Advocate in heaven. It is only the terminology which is different.

You are slow to learn. You need milk, not solid food!

The writer complains that he cannot say more on this important subject because "you are slow to learn". The word translated "slow" means "lazy" or "sluggish"; it comes up again in 6:12, "We do not want you to become lazy, but to imitate those who through faith and patience inherit what has been promised". Never far from the writer's mind is the danger of forfeiting the promised inheritance through laziness – not so much the deliberate renunciation of the faith as a gradual falling away through laziness and indifference.

They needed someone to teach them all over again the elementary truths, the rudiments of God's word. Some of these basic doctrines are listed in 6:1-2. The same word is used in Galatians 4 and Colossians 2 of "beggarly elements" or "miserable principles" to be avoided at all costs, but here they are the basic truths of the Christian faith, the milk of God's word, which by now they should have been familiar with.

Paul has the same complaint against the Corinthians. They too were babes in Christ, fleshly people who were simply not ready for solid food, but only milk (1 Corinthians 3:1-4). Their salvation was not at risk but some of them would be saved "only as one escaping through the flames" (3:15). This low level of belief and commitment was prevalent among the Hebrews as well. Probably in every age there have been large numbers of lazy waverers, infants "not acquainted with the teaching about righteousness". That is certainly the case at the present time. May we at least be found among those who persevere, "so that when you have done the will of God, you will receive what he has promised" (10:36).

Going on to maturity
Hebrews 6:1-12

Perfection/maturity is one of the key words of this epistle. Christ Himself was made perfect through suffering (5:9; 7:28), and through His one sacrifice He has made perfect for ever those who have been made holy (10:14). He has in mind the Old Testament saints especially (11:40; 12:23), though perfection is also the aim and destiny of Christians today 6:1; 11:40). The Law, on the other hand, makes nothing perfect (7:19; 9:9; 10:1).

Those addressed here are urged to leave behind the elementary teachings about Christ and to go on to maturity. Six items of elementary teaching are mentioned. They are all basic concepts, not even exclusively Christian though they had for Christians a wider application. They include: repentance from dead works (see 9:14), faith toward God, instruction about baptisms (that is ceremonial washings as in 9:10, though including no doubt Christian baptism), laying on of hands, resurrection of the dead, and eternal judgment. Pious Jews would have accepted all these tenets, which were the foundation of Christian belief as well. But a Christian who stopped at this point was in grave danger of losing the new insight provided by faith in Christ and of falling back into Judaism.

This danger, both here and throughout the epistle, is the most pressing concern of the writer. He never ceases to drive home the dire consequences of apostasy. Words and phrases such as the following abound: drifting away (2:1), ignoring/neglecting such a great salvation (2:3), hardened by the deceitfulness of sin, as in the rebellion (3:8,13), falling through disobedience (4:11), deliberately keeping on sinning (10:26), shrinking back and being destroyed (10:39).

The verses before us in 6:4-8 provide one of the most stark warnings to be found. It is *impossible*, he says, for those who have been enlightened (tasted the heavenly gift, shared in the Holy Spirit etc.) *if they fall away* to be brought back to repentance, because they are crucifying the Son of God all over again and subjecting Him to public disgrace.

The same warning is repeated in 10:26-31. "If we deliberately keep on sinning after we have received the knowledge of the truth, *no sacrifice for sins is left*, but only a fearful expectation of judgment and of raging fire that will consume the enemies of God."

What is he saying?

What should we make of these warnings? Is it possible, after all, to commit the unpardonable sin and to lose one's salvation completely and for ever? Many writers feel this is going too far.

> (1) The Israelites in the wilderness did not lose their salvation; they simply lost the opportunity of entering the Promised Land (3:11; 4:11).

> (2) Esau sold his birthright for a single meal. Though he sought the blessing with tears he could not bring about a change of mind. (12:16-17). It was however only his inheritance which he forfeited, not his salvation.

> (3) The land that produces thorns and thistles is worthless and in danger of being cursed, and its end is to be burnt (6:8). It is not however the land itself which is burnt, but the thorns and thistles growing thereon.

(4) Paul draws the same lesson from the example of the Israelites in the wilderness (1 Corinthians 10:1-13): "God was not pleased with most of them; their bodies were scattered over the desert…in one day 23,000 of them died." But Paul stops short of saying that their salvation was at stake. In fact he states the opposite: "…he himself will be saved, but only as one escaping through the flames" (1 Corinthians 3:15).

Should we therefore conclude that these Hebrew believers were not in danger of losing their salvation but only the things that accompany salvation (6:9)? Or conversely, should we give full force to the uncompromising language employed: "…it is *impossible* for those… to be brought back to repentance"; no sacrifice for sins is left?

We should give them their full force

In my judgment the writer means precisely what he says. But why should this be so? It is "because to their loss they are crucifying the Son of God all over again" (6:6); trampling the Son of God under foot (10:29).

It needs to be remembered that the Israelite nation at this time fell into two unequal sections. On the one hand the unbelieving majority faced an unenviable future because they had failed to recognise the time of their visitation and had crucified the Lord of glory. On the other hand the believing remnant could expect to enjoy God's favour and blessing. If however a professing believer were to renounce his faith in Christ and revert to Judaism, he must expect to share the fate of the majority. He had after all changed sides, and of his own volition had joined the unbelieving majority doomed to destruction.

Our Lord had the same type of person in mind in Matthew 7:21-23. "Not everyone who says to me, 'Lord, Lord,' will enter the kingdom of heaven, but only he who does the will of my Father who is in heaven. Many will say to me on that day, 'Lord, Lord, did we not prophesy in your name, and in your name drive out demons and perform many miracles?' Then I will tell them plainly, 'I never knew you. Away from me, you evildoers!'

What about us?

These sanctions may not apply to believers today, or even to Gentile believers at the time of writing. It is nevertheless a very serious matter to renege on one's Christian commitment. The loss is incalculable, inestimable. To drift back into an unbelieving mindset and lifestyle amounts to renouncing the faith. The remedy is to go on, "to show the same diligence (as you have already shown) to the very end, in order to make your hope sure" (Hebrews 6:11). The man who stands still cannot avoid sliding back. The Christian life is like riding a bicycle: you either go forward or you fall off!

Where then is our security?

The writer is confident that what he has been saying does not apply to those he is writing to. Moreover this confidence is well founded, as he says later on: "For by a single offering he has perfected for all time those who are being sanctified" (10:14). We can rest assured that we are "perfected for all time" since no true believer will renounce his faith as envisaged in 6:4-6 (1 John 2:19; 3:9). See also the section on Hebrews 10:26-39.

Priest in the Order of Melchizedek Hebrews 6:13-7:28

When God made a promise to Abraham, since He had no-one greater by whom to swear, He swore by Himself, saying, "I will surely bless you and give you many descendants." The reference is to Genesis 22:16-17 where the Lord swears by Himself that He will bless Abraham and make his descendants as numerous as the stars and the sand. The occasion was Abraham's willingness to sacrifice his son. It was because he had shown such sacrificial obedience in not withholding his son, his only son. It is therefore by two unchangeable things – the oath and the promise – that we who have fled for refuge might have strong encouragement to seize the hope set before us.

Here, however, the writer is thinking more especially of the promise to which reference is made in 5:6. This was also confirmed by an oath (in which it is impossible for God to lie): "You are a priest for ever, in the order of Melchizedek" (Psalm 110:4). We have this hope as an anchor for the soul, firm and secure, which enters the inner sanctuary "behind the curtain". The curtain corresponds to Christ's human body, His flesh (10:20). By His death on the cross He opened for us a new and living way "through the curtain" into the Most Holy Place. This is the heavenly reality which was typified by the holy place in the sanctuary. Here He has become on our behalf a High Priest for ever after the order of Melchizedek. The writer has now returned to the point, 5:10, from which he digresses in 5:11-6:12.

Melchizedek compared with Christ Hebrews 7

The seventh chapter of Hebrews is so straightforward it hardly needs comment. There are two themes, one of comparison and the other of contrast. In the first place Christ is compared with Melchizedek and is shown to correspond remarkably closely with what is said of him. In the second place He is contrasted with the Levitical priesthood and shown to be its opposite in every detail. His similarity to Melchizedek is shown in the following comparisons: -

Melchizedek	Christ
King of Salem which means "King of Peace" (1-2)	He was also "King of Peace"
"King of Righteousness" (2)	As was Christ
Priest of God Most High (1)	Priest of the order of Melchizedek
Without father or mother, beginning of days or end of life (3)	Priest on the basis of the power of the indestructible life (16)
He remains a priest for ever (3)	Like the Son of God (3)
Greater than Abraham (4, 7)	As was Christ
Did not trace his descent from Levi (6)	Nor did Christ
Blessed him who had the promises (6)	Through Him the seed of Abraham is richly blessed

Christ's priesthood is after the order of Melchizedek, a priesthood different in every respect from that associated with Levi.

The Levitical priesthood inferior in every way

Levitical	Christ
No perfection attainable (11)	The Son Made Perfect for ever (28)
No-one from Judah ever served (13)	Descended from Judah (14)
On the basis of an ancestral law (16)	On the basis of an indestructible life (16)
Weak and useless, making nothing perfect (18-19)	A better hope by which we draw near to God (19)
Became priests without an oath (20)	Not without an oath! Hence the guarantee of a better covenant (20-22)
Many priests because of death (23)	Jesus lives for ever, hence a permanent priesthood and complete salvation. He always lives to intercede for them (24-25)
They offer sacrifices day after day first for their own sins... (27)	He sacrificed for their sins once for all when He offered Himself (27)
The law appoints high priests who are weak (28)	The oath appointed the Son who has been made perfect for ever (28)

The long and short of it is that we have a high priest who meets our need, one who is holy, blameless, pure, set apart from sinners, exalted above the heavens. **Indeed what a Saviour!**

The New Covenant
Hebrews 8

The similarities and differences between the Aaronic priesthood
and that of Christ can be set out in parallel columns as in my last
article.

Aaron's priesthood	Christ
They serve a copy and shadow of the heavenly things	A minister in the holy places in the true tent that the Lord set up, not man
Appointed to offer gifts and sacrifices	This priest also has something to offer
They offer gifts according to the law	He would not be a priest at all on earth
Their ministry is old	His ministry is so much more excellent
They serve the old covenant	He mediates a better covenant since it is enacted on better promises

The gifts and sacrifices which the high priest was appointed to offer
are defined in chapter 5:1 as "gifts and sacrifices for sins". The
something which Christ had to offer was also for sins. This
sacrifice He did "once for all when he offered up himself" (7:27).
It is "the blood of Christ, who through the eternal Spirit offered
himself without blemish to God" (9:14).

The Tabernacle

Moses made everything according to the pattern or model that was shown him on the Mount. This included the very boards of the Tabernacle as well as the entire superstructure and everything in it. Indeed, every detail was included in this plan (Exodus 25:40; 26:30; 27:8). This blueprint or archetype was something more than a diagram or written instruction, it was a visible representation which Moses copied to the last detail.

The Tabernacle in the wilderness was "a copy and shadow of the heavenly things". Many have found much of interest in Tabernacle typology and symbolism, though it is certainly not everyone's 'cup of tea'. But for those so inclined it has proved a most instructive discipline, and there are many books to guide the earnest inquirer. The one I like best is called *Tabernacle Types and Teachings*, edited by W. S. Martin and A. Marshall (1924).

The new covenant

There follows next a long quotation from Jeremiah 31:31-34 all about the new covenant.[2] He does not mention Jeremiah by name but quotes him almost word for word. The following points should be noted about the new covenant.

1. It will be made "with the house of Israel and with the house of Judah", as both Jeremiah and Hebrews make clear. This decisively excludes Gentile believers who generally speaking like to think of themselves as coming under the umbrella of this covenant. Its chief function is to supersede the old covenant "made with their fathers"

---

[2] For more on the New Covenant see *More on Hebrews*, the last chapter of this book.

at the Exodus. This being the case, it must of necessity apply to the same people or it would fail in its purpose.

2. It is a unilateral covenant, God being the only active participant. In this respect it contrasts with the old covenant which was bilateral, imposing obligations on both parties. If the operative words of the old covenant were "if you" (Exodus 19:5, Deuteronomy 30:16), those of the new covenant are "I will". "I will" occurs six times in vv. 10-12 (Jeremiah 31:33-34). It is therefore a covenant of promise like the covenant made with Abraham.

> I will make a new covenant with the house of Israel and the house of Judah." (Jeremiah 31:31)

3. The most important feature of the new covenant is stated first. "I will put my laws into their minds, and write them on their hearts." The old covenant had failed because the Israelites had been unable to keep the law. The new one will succeed because the law will then be written on the fleshy tables of the heart. "What was needed was a new nature, a heart liberated from its bondage to sin, a heart which not only spontaneously knew and loved the will of God but had the power to do it" (Bruce). The people are still under the same obligation to obey the law but with this difference, that they now have the motivation and ability to do so.

Was this something new?

But was not this already true for Acts period believers and even for faithful Jews in pre-Christian times? There was certainly an application of the new covenant in the Acts period (2 Corinthians 3; Romans 2:29), and even in the Old Testament there were those who had the law in their hearts (Psalm 37:31, 40:8, Isaiah 51:7, Psalm 119). But only when the new covenant is established at the second coming of Christ will this be the experience of the entire nation. Once more in covenant relationship with their God (10), known by and knowing the Lord (11), their sins forgiven and forgotten (12), there will be no excuse or occasion for the failure of the past.

The Old Covenant
Hebrews 9:1-14

Hebrews 9 falls into two halves, vv. 1-14 dealing with the old covenant[3] and its deficiencies and vv. 15-28 dealing with the new covenant, explaining its superiority and sufficiency. In this article I shall look briefly at the old covenant and its regulations.

The Tabernacle

The wilderness tabernacle consisted of two "tents" as described here. The first tent is called Holy (or Holy Place) and the second tent Holy of Holies. This tent was situated "after the second veil". This veil is the Temple veil said to be rent "from top to bottom" when the Lord Jesus yielded up His spirit (Matthew 27:51; Mark 15:38). It has already been mentioned in Hebrews 6:19 as marking the entrance into the inner sanctuary where we have a sure and steadfast anchor of the soul "behind the curtain"; and is identified in 10:20 with Christ's flesh which like the veil was rent on the cross, thereby opening up "the new and living way". According to Josephus, "This veil was very ornamental, and embroidered with all sorts of flowers which the earth produces; and there were interwoven into it all sorts of variety that might be an ornament, excepting the forms of animals" (*Antiquities* VI.3.4).

The contents of the tents

Three things are mentioned as being present in the first tent: the

---

[3] For more on the Old Covenant see *More on Hebrews*, the last chapter of this book.

lampstand, the table and the bread of the presence (lit. "the setting forth of the loaves"). These speak of light and sustenance which are now available in Christ (John 6:35; 8:12). Under the old covenant, however, the light was dim and shadowy and the showbread inaccessible except to the priests (Matthew 12:4).

In the second tent seven things are mentioned: the censer, the Ark of the Covenant, the urn holding the manna, Aaron's staff that budded, the tables of the covenant, the cherubim of glory, and the mercy seat. The first of these is translated "altar of incense" in modern versions, but the altar of incense was not situated in the inner sanctuary (Exodus 30:6), and *thumiaterion* in the Septuagint is used of the censer but never of the incense altar (2 Chronicles 26:19; Ezekiel 8:11). It was indeed close to the second veil and could be said to belong to the inner sanctuary (1 Kings 6:22), but it certainly was not in it as Josephus confirms (*Antiquities* III.6.8). According to him it was situated between the lampstand and the table of showbread in the holy place.

Most of these were made of gold and they speak of Christ, His person and things associated with Him. For example, the ark containing the tables of the covenant is a striking symbol of Christ who could say, "I desire to do your will, O my God, your law is within my heart" (Psalm 40:8). But we cannot here enlarge on these types and shadows any more than the writer of Hebrews.

The old order

The writer makes the following points with reference to the old order (9:6-10). (1) The way into the Holy of Holies was closed. Even the high priest was permitted to enter only once a year. (2) He could not go in "without blood", for "without the shedding of blood there is no forgiveness of sins" (22). (3) His gifts and sacrifices had no power to perfect the conscience of the worshipper. This word "perfect" is an important one in Hebrews. It is emphasized that the law could make no-one perfect (7:19; 9:9; 10:1), but that Christ by His one offering has perfected for all time those who are sanctified (10:14). Only in resurrection will perfection be finally realised in the experience of believers, and this will happen more or less simultaneously for Old and New Testament believers at the second coming of Christ (11:40; 1 Thessalonians 4:13-18).

But Christ

It is with relief that we read these words in v. 11. What the law could not do Christ has done once and for all. He has entered into the holies, not by means of the blood of goats and calves but by means of His own blood, thus securing an eternal redemption (12). The blood of goats and bulls and the ashes of the red heifer (Numbers 19) may have availed to purify the flesh, but **how much more** does the blood of Christ purify our conscience from dead works to serve the living God! The scapegoat had failed to take away Israel's sin after some 1500 attempts, but Christ bore away the sins of the world at the first attempt, "once for all" on the cross of Calvary.

The "how much mores" of Scripture deserve careful attention. See Matthew 7:11, Luke 11:13; 12:24,28, Romans 11:12,24, Hebrews 10:29 ("how much worse punishment"!).

The New Covenant
Hebrews 9:15-28

Hebrews 9:15 begins, "Therefore He is the mediator of a new covenant." Why? Because He has secured an eternal redemption with His own blood ... the blood of Christ, who through the eternal Spirit offered Himself without blemish to God (9:14).

The *NIV* continues, "In the case of a will, it is necessary to prove the death of the one who made it, because a will is in force only when somebody has died; it never takes effect while the one who made it is living. This is why even the first covenant ..." This translation is representative. Even the *KJV* renders here "testament" rather than "covenant", though the word is the same. There has been much discussion on this point since many have felt that to translate *diatheke* by will or testament in this place is inconsistent (if not incongruous) with the rest of the epistle.

A literal translation of v. 16 would be, "For where there is a covenant there must of necessity be the death of the appointed one to be brought." Too much attention has been placed on the word *diatheke* which is invariably translated "covenant" in both the Septuagint and the New Testament (with the exception of this passage and Galatians 3:15). The words translated "appointed" and "to be brought" deserve far more attention.

The word "appointed" is the verbal noun from which "covenant" is derived, and is usually understood to mean "covenant-maker". But the primary meaning of the word is "appoint", as in Luke 22:29, "As my Father *appointed* a kingdom for me, so do I *appoint* for you." The appointed one in Hebrews cannot be the covenant-maker, but rather the appointed victim to be brought as an offering. To bring or offer is frequently the sense of *phero* in the Septuagint, as for example in Genesis 4:3-4 (its first occurrence): "Cain *brought* of the fruit of the earth a sacrifice to the Lord. And Abel *brought* the firstborn of his sheep." The passive infinitive "to be brought" shows that the appointed one was brought by someone else, rather than offered by himself as was Christ.

The sacrifice appointed when God covenanted with Abraham is described in Genesis 15. That required when He covenanted with Israel at Sinai is described in Exodus 24 and here in Hebrews 9:18-21. So also was a sacrifice appointed in order to secure the new covenant, namely the shed blood of Christ.

Hebrews 9 does not speak of the death of the covenant-maker but the death of the covenant victim. But the word has been chosen with care since *diathemenos* would naturally suggest the covenant-maker (as it has to most translators), and in this instance the appointed victim was in fact the covenant-maker Himself. But covenant-maker is not the primary meaning here, since "it simply is not true to say that 'where a covenant is, there must of necessity be the death of him that made it' "F.F. Bruce). But once it is recognised that *diathemenos* refers primarily to the appointed victim there is no further difficulty. Covenant keeps its meaning of covenant as in the rest of this epistle and the Bible as a whole.

The blood of Christ

Some people are offended by what they see as a distasteful preoccupation with blood in the Bible. But the necessity of blood is due entirely to the universality of sin. "Indeed, under the law almost everything is purified with blood, and without the shedding of blood there is no forgiveness of sins" (22). The last clause seems to mirror Leviticus 17:11, "It is the blood that makes atonement by reason of the life (soul)."

The Levitical sacrifices sufficed to purify the copies of the heavenly things, but what about the heavenlies themselves? These were purified with better sacrifices, namely the real and personal sacrifice of Christ (23). Even the heavenlies are not pure in God's eyes, and He puts no trust in His holy ones (Job 15:15). The word for "heavenlies" is the same as in Ephesians ("in the heavenly places"). It would seem that spiritual forces of evil have infiltrated even this exalted sphere (Ephesians 6:12), and our presence there cannot but defile it more.

He will appear a second time

At first sight the comparison in vv. 27-28 seems a trifle illogical. "Just as it is appointed for men to die once, and after that to face the judgment, so Christ has been offered once to take away the sins of many people; and he will appear a second time, not to bear sin, but to bring salvation to those who are waiting for him."

But how, one wonders, can salvation be parallel to judgment? The point is surely that Christ has already taken away the sins of the many, so that when He returns there is no fearful expectation of judgment for them, but simply the joyful fulfilment of their salvation. As our Lord said of the one who believes in Him, "he does not come into judgment, but has passed from death into life" (John 5:24).

Sacrifices and offerings you have not desired
Hebrews 10:1-25

Our standard versions have mistranslated the first verse of Hebrews 10. Westcott and Welch have argued for this though Bruce is apparently unconvinced. It is the word translated "endlessly" in the *NIV* and "continuously" in the *KJV* and other versions which is wrongly placed. This should be joined to the words which follow it rather than to those which precede it. Hence it should be translated, "It (the law) can never, by the same sacrifices which they offer every year, *in perpetuity* perfect the ones approaching." Compare this with the translation in your own Bible.

We know this to be correct from the positive statement in v. 14, "For by one offering He has perfected *in perpetuity* those being sanctified." How can perfection be obtained, *perfection in perpetuity*, that is the question. The law with its repeatedly offered sacrifices is incapable of doing any such thing, but Christ by His one offering on the cross has *perfected for ever* those who come to Him. "In perpetuity" is emphasized in v. 1 by being placed at the head of the clause.

There are two other places where these words occur in Hebrews. These are 7:3, "resembling the Son of God, he (Melchizedek) continues a priest *for ever*"; and 10:12, "But when this priest (Christ) had offered *for all time* one sacrifice for sins, he sat down at the right hand of God." The translation "endlessly/ continuously" is clearly out of place. "In perpetuity/ for all time" is what is required.

Here again it is emphasized that Christ, by His one offering, has achieved what the law with its repeated offerings year after year could never achieve. These offerings were unable to cleanse *the conscience* (9:9; 10:2). But the blood of Christ does purify the conscience from dead works (9:14), "our hearts sprinkled clean from an evil conscience" (10:22). On the day of Atonement there was "a *remembrance* of sin year after year" (10:3), but under the new covenant there is not even the remembrance of sins (10:17).

"Lo, I have come to do thy will, O God"

The quotation in vv. 5-7 is derived from Psalm 40:6-8 (*LXX* Psalm 39). They are the words of David in the original, but here they are appropriated by Christ. He it was who spoke through David and here He recites His own words. "Sacrifice and offering thou hast not desired, but a body hast thou prepared for me..." The Old Testament writers knew that God took no real delight in animal sacrifices. What He really wanted was *obedience* (1 Samuel 15:22; Jeremiah 7:22-23), a broken spirit and a contrite heart (Psalm 51:17), justice, kindness and humility (Micah 6:6-8; Amos 5:21-24). Here, in Psalm 40, Christ in total obedience offers Himself: "Lo, I come to do thy will, O God."

He offered His own body as the once-for-all sacrifice for sin (5,10), in place of the oft-repeated ineffective sacrifices in which the Lord took no delight.

And having done that, "He sat down at the right hand of God" (12). The priests were perpetually standing, their work never finished. In the Temple no provision was made for sitting; chairs or seats are not even mentioned. But Christ, "when he had made purification for sins, sat down at the right hand of the Majesty on high" (1:3; 8:1; 10:12; 12:2), there to remain until His enemies should submit to His authority.

"Let us..." (19-25)

This section concludes with three exhortations beginning with "Let us". "Let us draw near with a true heart in full assurance of faith" (22); "Let us hold fast the confession of our hope without wavering" (23); "Let us consider how to stir up one another to love and good works."

These correspond to faith, hope and love. We have faith in "the new and living way" that has been opened up for us "through the curtain" by the blood of Jesus.

We can hold fast to the confession of our hope (the better hope, 7:19) without wavering, for He who has promised is faithful. And we can encourage one another into an intense desire (lit. *paroxysm*) for love and good works.

This will require mutual encouragement in their regular gathering for worship -- which on no account should be allowed to slip; and all the more so as they see the Day approaching. This is the day when "in a little while" the Coming One will come and will not delay (10:37).

What if we sin deliberately after having believed? Hebrews 10:26-39

A subject which repeatedly comes up in this epistle, either by inference or plain statement, is the writer's fear that some of his readers were in grave danger of falling back into a conventional Judaism, at the same time deliberately renouncing their faith in Christ. This concern came to the fore in chapter 6:1-8. He said there, "it is impossible to restore again to repentance those who have been enlightened, who have tasted the heavenly gift ... if they then fall away, since they are crucifying once again the Son of God to their own harm and holding him up to contempt."

Commenting on that passage I expressed the opinion that those who fell away and joined ranks with unbelieving Judaism would suffer the same fate as those who never believed. I still incline to that opinion, though having read what Lang and Welch have to say on the subject I can see the strength of their point of view. The best that I can do is to present the arguments and leave the reader to make up his own mind.

He is writing to believers

From the passage just referred to in Hebrews 6 it is certain that those addressed were, at the time of writing, genuine believers at least to outward appearance. They had been enlightened, tasted the heavenly gift, shared in the Holy Spirit, tasted the goodness of the word of God and the powers of the age to come (6:5). In chapter 10 he says "you were enlightened" (32), and adds other indications of Christian commitment. They had received the knowledge (*epignosis*, experimental knowledge) of the truth (26); they had been sanctified by the blood of the covenant (29); they had been exposed to persecution and abuse (32, 33); they had shown compassion on those in prison, and accepted joyfully the plundering of their property, knowing that they had a better and lasting possession (34). High commendation indeed!

The danger which confronted them

They were nevertheless in danger of sinning *willfully* (26), that is sinning "with a high hand" (Numbers 15:30,31) for which no atonement was provided by the law of Moses . By so doing they would *trample on* the Son of God, and treat the blood of the covenant as *a common thing* -- like that of any other man (29). They would *outrage* the Spirit of grace, "crucifying again for themselves the Son of God and putting him to open shame" (6:6). A truly fearful indictment! It hardly seems possible that any true believer, let alone those so highly commended, could fall away so dreadfully -- but cases can be cited.

The punishment envisaged

For such there "no longer remains a sacrifice for sins" but only "a fearful expectation of judgment, and a fury of fire that will consume the adversaries" (26-27). This is an allusion to Isaiah 26:11. Examples of the fire that consumes the adversaries include the following:

(1) Nadab and Abihu who offered unauthorized fire before the Lord, and "fire came out from before the Lord and

consumed them" (Leviticus 10:2).

(2) Korah, Dathan and Abiram, and the 250 chiefs who rebelled against Moses. "Fire came out from the Lord and consumed the 250 men offering the incense" (Numbers 16:35).

(3) Achan and family. "They burned them with fire and stoned them with stones" (Joshua 7:15,25).

(4) In the New Testament we think of Ananias and Sapphira who "fell down and breathed their last" at the word of Peter (Acts 5).

All these suffered *temporal* death by fire or some other means, but there is no reason to suppose that their eternal salvation was forfeited. Like those mentioned in 1 Corinthians 3:15, they themselves will be saved, but only as through fire. If this is the punishment implied in Hebrews 10, the ultimate salvation of those found guilty may not be in dispute.

It is indeed "a fearful thing to fall into the hands of the living God" (31). When David chose to "fall into the hands of the Lord, for his mercy is great" (2 Samuel 24:14), 70,000 people died in only three days though David himself was spared. A terrible retribution is implied, but not necessarily an eternal one.

Those who shrink back are destroyed

In v. 39 he says, "We are not of those who shrink back *to destruction*." Arguably the word *apoleia* does not always mean final destruction. Speaking of those who live as enemies of the cross of Christ, Paul says, "Their end is destruction, their god is their belly, and they glory in their shame, with minds set on earthly things" (Philippians 3:19).

If he is speaking here of carnal Christians (as seems to be the case), their ultimate salvation is nevertheless assured.

Verse 39 continues, "... but of those who have faith to the possession of the soul." The same (or related) words all occur in Luke 17:33, "Whoever seeks to *possess* his *soul* will *lose* it, but whoever *loses* (his soul) will preserve it." This comes immediately after the words "Remember Lot's wife!" Lot's wife is a tragic example of someone who shrank back to destruction and a warning to anyone tempted to do the same. But Lot's wife may still be finally saved.

Where do we go from here?

A strong case can be made for the view that the punishment indicated in Hebrews 6 and 10 is essentially of a temporal nature and that the ultimate security of the saints, even if they wilfully abandon the faith and trample on the Son of God, is not necessarily affected. But all the cases of temporal judgment that can be cited do not settle the matter, for it says in v. 29, "*How much more* punishment do you think will be deserved by the one who has trampled on the Son of God...?" His punishment will evidently be *worse* than those mentioned -- but how much worse? That is the question to which we would like an answer, but no conclusive answer is given!

The testimony of John

John seems to have in mind the same sort of people in his first epistle. In 2:19 he says, "They went out from us, but they were not of us; for *if they had been of us, they would have continued with us. But they went out, that it might become plain that they all are not* of us". He continues, "Who is a liar but he who denies that Jesus is the Christ? ... No one who denies the Son has the Father" (22-23). See also 1 John 3:9-10.

Those commended for their faith.
Abel, Enoch and Noah
Hebrews 11:1-7

Hebrews 11 is the great chapter on Faith, just as 1 Corinthians 13 is the great chapter on Love. Arguably Hebrews 11 is the great chapter on Hope as well, since faith and hope go together and "faith is the assurance of things hoped for" (v.1). Love is the greatest of the three since it reaches out to other people, but faith and hope are equally important if one aspires to live a life well-pleasing to God.

The context

It is easy to forget that Hebrews 11 has a context and a homiletic purpose. The purpose is to impress on these wavering Hebrew believers, who were tempted to give up the struggle, the necessity to exercise their God-given faith and to persevere in the race which confronted them. To this effect he says in 12:1-2, "let us also lay aside every weight, and sin which clings so closely, and let us run with endurance the race that is set before us, looking to Jesus ..." The many examples of unflinching faith recorded in this chapter are designed to demonstrate what faith can achieve and how it motivated their national heroes.

What is faith?

Faith, we are told, is the assurance, grounds, guarantee (lit. "that which underlies") of things hoped for, the proof of things not seen. Things hoped for, things unseen, cannot be known apart from faith, but what is the basis of faith itself? According to Romans 10:17, "faith comes from hearing, and hearing through the word of Christ." Faith is believing the word of God, and faith-obedience is acting on what God has said. Examples of faith in action abound in the annals of the Old Testament and the Christian church. Cases well known to these Hebrew believers are here displayed for their encouragement and instruction.

The ages

"By faith we understand the ages to have been adjusted by a word of God." In this way the first clause of v. 3 is translated in my interlinear. It is certainly the ages (*aiones*, aeons) which are referred to, not the world or worlds, and it is their adjustment or preparation, not their creation. It is the same verb translated "prepared" in 10:5 ("a body hast thou prepared for me") and "equip" in 13:21 ("may the God of peace ... equip you with everything good that you may do his will"). The ages were perfectly prepared and equipped by God, and this we know from His word.

We are not thinking of geological ages (ice, stone etc.) as conceived by the world, but the ages and dispensations as conceived by God. There was a time "before the ages" (1 Corinthians 2:7) and there are "ages to come" (Ephesians 2:7) stretching into the limitless future, but all are prepared and arranged by God, fixed as their length and character. God made the ages (Hebrews 1:2), and there is a purpose of the ages (Ephesians 3:11) for which our only source of information is the Bible. Christ has appeared once for all at the completion of the ages (Hebrews 9:26), and the powers of the coming age were already at work (6:5).

It is important to understand that the things seen and experienced have not come into bein from observable phenomena, but have all been arranged by the word, will and wisdom of God. This first example of faith concerns "what is seen" as opposed to "the things not being seen" as mentioned in v. 1.

Abel

Abel offered a greater (or better) sacrifice than Cain. But in what respect was Abel's better? Was it that Abel brought a blood sacrifice whereas Cain brought the product of his labour and sweat? But Cain, surely, did right in bringing the fruit of the ground since that was his occupation.

The difference between them was in their attitude. Cain's offering was perfunctory and begrudging. Whereas Abel offered the *firstborn* of his flock and of their fat portions, Cain offered only the fruit of the ground, not even the *firstfruit*. It is implied that Cain did not do well, and that he too would be accepted if he availed himself of the sin-offering which even then was crouching at the door of their place of worship (Genesis 4:7). Maybe he should have brought a sin-offering as well as the firstfruit of the ground since this requirement was already well established.

God bore witness over Abel's gifts. He did so no doubt by consuming them with fire from heaven as on other occasions (Leviticus 9:24; Judges 6:21; 13:20 etc.). Abel's faith exemplifies the beginning of the Christian life, the assurance of righteousness through the blood of Christ. This is where the life of faith begins, and Abel's faith still speaks in that regard.

Enoch

From acceptance we move on to well-pleasing. Enoch is a fine example of someone who was well-pleasing to God. Genesis says that Enoch walked with God, after begetting Methuselah, for 300 years, and that "Enoch walked with God, and he was not, for God took him" (Genesis 5:22-24). In both places the Septuagint says that Enoch was well-pleasing to God, and it clarifies v. 24 by saying "and he was not found, because God translated him" (as in Hebrews).

Enoch was rewarded for his well-pleasing walk with God (for more than 300 years!) by being removed, taken up to heaven, without seeing death. For this to happen he must have been "changed": his corruptible nature must have put on incorruption and his mortal nature immortality (1 Corinthians 15:51-54). This is precisely what these Hebrew believers could expect for themselves if they cultivated a well-pleasing walk with the Lord, for God is the great Rewarder (*Misthapodotes*) of those who earnestly seek Him (6). This follows on from 10:35 where they were urged not to throw away their confidence which has "great reward" (*misthapodosia*, full payment of wages).

Noah

Faith is the proof of things not seen. Noah was warned concerning things not seen and then obeyed God's unusual instructions to the letter. He built an immense boat-like container on dry land hundreds of miles from the sea! By this he condemned the world, who saw what he was doing and ridiculed him for his crazy behaviour and even crazier warning of impending doom. He nevertheless persevered for what may have been a hundred years, despising the shame.

Abel had received witness that he was righteous by faith (4). Enoch was translated because of his well-pleasing walk with God (5). Noah became an heir of the righteousness which is by faith (7).

Noah's bold and fearless obedience to God's strange command is the antidote to all those who would "shrink back to their destruction" (10:39); while the fate of the unbelieving world at that time is a stark warning to any who might be tempted to fall away after receiving knowledge of the truth.

Those commended for their faith.
Abraham and Sarah
Hebrews 11:8-16

"By faith **Abraham** obeyed." The two words *faith* and *obey* are inseparable (e.g. Romans 1:5; 16:26). While still in Ur of the Chaldees Abraham heard the Lord's command, "Go out from your land and from your kindred into the land that I will show you" (Acts 7:3). Accompanied by his father and other family members he got as far as Haran in north Syria, but there they settled down. Terah seems to have been the stumbling-block: he refused to go any further. Then, after Terah's death, Abraham heard the command again, "Go ... to the land that I will show you" (Genesis 12:1). So Abraham set out not knowing where he was to go (Hebrews 11:8).

He had the promise that he would receive an inheritance, but was not told what it was. Only after his separation from Lot was he shown precisely what his inheritance would be (Genesis 13:14-18). But in fact he never received a square foot of it (Acts 7:5). He lived there as in a foreign land, living in tents with Isaac and Jacob, joint-heirs of the same promise (Hebrews 11:9).

Joint-heirs

Isaac and Jacob were not simply Abraham's heirs (as you might expect), but joint-heirs with Abraham himself. This they were because the same promise was granted to each of them in turn:

Abraham (Genesis 13:15; 17:8), Isaac (26:3), Jacob (28:13; 35:12). They were therefore joint-heirs on a basis of equality. The same word is used in Ephesians 3:6 of the joint-heirship of Jew and Gentile in the body of Christ. This also is a joint-heirship on the basis of equality: no group or denomination has precedence over any other, whatever they may think!

The city which has foundations

How did Abraham cope with this nomadic existence, without house or homeland, living in tents with Isaac and Jacob? He accepted it willingly, even joyfully, "for he looked to the city which has foundations, whose builder and maker is God" (11:10). He and his descendants did not yearn for an earthly commonwealth, for they desired a better country, that is a heavenly one (16). There is no way they could have known about this city except by revelation. But having received this revelation they embraced it by faith. They recognized that they too were strangers and sojourners on the earth, whose true homeland belonged to another country altogether (13).

The readers of this epistle would have had no trouble identifying with Abraham. They had joyfully accepted the plundering of their property in the sure knowledge that they had a better possession and an abiding one (10:34). They too had come to Mount Zion, to the city of the living God, the heavenly Jerusalem (12:22). What a boost to their faith it must have been to be told that Abraham, Isaac and Jacob had experienced the same deprivation and abiding hope as themselves!

By faith Sarah

"By faith Sarah herself received power to conceive, even when she was past age, since she considered him faithful who had promised" (Hebrews 11:11). But the *NIV* says, "By faith *Abraham*, even though *he* was past age ..." What right have the *NIV*, *NRSV* and others to replace Sarah by Abraham -- an unwarranted liberty, surely? The reason is given by F.F. Bruce: "The phrase translated 'to conceive seed' just does not mean that; it refers to the father's part in the generative process, not the mother's. A literal translation would be 'for the deposition of seed'; it does not denote the receiving or conception of seed."

Bruce suggests that the words "Sarah herself" should be understood as datives rather than nominatives, and the sense, "By faith (Abraham) also, together with Sarah, received power to beget a child when he was past age..." This clearly is the rationale behind the *NIV* translation.

But "deposition of seed" is not the only possible translation. Everywhere else *katabole* means "foundation" and *sperma* (when used of human seed) means "offspring" or "family". The meaning is therefore, "By faith Sarah herself received strength for *founding a family*." One could almost say "to start a family". But this was no ordinary family; it was the family of promise, the seed of Abraham and Sarah.

It is true that Sarah found the idea quite laughable to begin with (Genesis 18:9-15). But having been rebuked for her unbelief she evidently received it by faith. She was another for whom faith was the assurance of things hoped for, the proof of things not seen.

Those commended for their faith. Abraham, Isaac, Jacob, Joseph Hebrews 11:17-22

Most of the tenses in this chapter are aorists. There are however three examples of the perfect tense. The perfect tense describes a past event whose action is carried on to the present time. A good example is the statement in 12:2 that Jesus *has sat down* at the right hand of God. He sat down in the past and is still seated today, past and present. The first of the three in Hebrews 11 was at v. 6 where it says of Enoch that *he has obtained witness* to have been well-pleasing to God. Enoch obtained witness that he was well-pleasing and that witness still remains.

By faith Abraham

"Abraham, being tested, *has offered up* Isaac, and *was offering up* his only begotten son" (17). The tenses are instructive: a perfect tense followed by an imperfect or past continuous. It is implied that Abraham's offering of Isaac was a continuing event whose repercussions were still felt long after it happened. And that indeed proved to be the case. From this story generations of believers have received a profound insight into the heart of God -- what it meant to God the Father to send His only-begotten Son to die on the cross. Even more so than Abel's, Abraham's faith-obedience is still speaking today to all those who have ears to hear.

By faith Isaac

"By faith Isaac blessed Jacob and Esau concerning things to come."
One thinks initially of the shameful and compromising charade
described in Genesis 27 when Jacob stole his brother's blessing by
deceit. But on that occasion there was no faith on Isaac's part, only
disobedience and shame. He must have known the Lord's word
uttered before the twins were born: "the older shall serve the
younger" (25:23), but he chose instead to bless the elder, the son
whom he loved. And why did he love Esau? Because he did eat of
his venison! (25:28)

When he discovered what Jacob had done, he trembled
exceedingly. Again, there was no faith in that, only guilt and alarm.
It was not till Jacob was about to leave for Paddan-Aram that Isaac
exercised true faith by blessing Jacob (28:3-4) – a blessing which
the Lord confirmed in 35:11 when Jacob's name was changed to
Israel. Isaac overcame his natural affection for Esau and his disgust
and resentment at Jacob's deceit, and he acted in obedience to the
Lord's revealed will and purpose.

By faith Jacob

In similar circumstances Jacob blessed the two sons of Joseph
(Genesis 48). Here also the father was old and nearly blind. Again
two sons were involved, and the younger son was blessed above
the elder contrary to his father's wishes.

Prior to this event Jacob worshipped leaning on the top of his staff
(47:31) This also was an act of faith since Joseph had just sworn to
his father to bury him in the family burial place in the land of
Canaan. In this way Jacob demonstrated his faith in God's word

and his assurance of things hoped for. The *NIV* correctly changes "bed" to "staff" in this v. (47:31), in line with the Septuagint and Hebrews (*matteh* for *mittah*, a pointing error by the Massoretes).

By faith Joseph

Of the many heroic and faithful deeds performed by Joseph during his marvellous career, the only things recorded are his mentioning (or remembrance) of the Exodus and instructions respecting his bones. His words are recorded at the end of Genesis (50:24-25). As with his predecessors, Joseph's final words expressed his faith in God's promise, his assurance of things hoped for and his conviction of things not seen. This, it would seem, is the kind of faith which God especially approves of, our belief of His word about the hereafter, a subject in the nature of the case outside the realm of sight or reason.

Those commended for their faith
Moses
Hebrews 11:23-28

"By faith Moses, when he was born, was hidden for three months by his parents, because they saw that the child was fair." A mother's desire to save her baby because it is beautiful speaks of parental love and compassion rather than faith. The book of Exodus does not throw much light on the matter. We are there told that Moses' mother, "when she saw that he was good (or pleasing), hid him for three months" (2:2). More enlightening is Acts 7:20 where we are informed that Moses was "fair *to God.*"

Moses was not simply pleasing to his parents, he was pleasing *to God.* His parents, Amram and Jochebed, must have been told by God that their son was a very special child and that they were to hide him in the way they did. It is their faith, shown in their hiding Moses for three months in defiance of Pharaoh's decree, which is here acclaimed.

Amram and Jochebed were both very old when Moses was born. He was almost certainly an answer to prayer like John the Baptist.

By faith Moses

"By faith Moses, when he was grown up (lit. "become great"), refused to be called the son of Pharaoh's daughter, choosing rather to be ill-treated with the people of God than to have, even for a time, the enjoyment of sin. He considered reproach for Christ greater riches than the treasures of Egypt, for he was looking for the reward (*misthapodosia*). (11:24-25)

Already we have been told in this chapter that God is the Rewarder *(Misthapodotes)* of those who seek Him (6). And in 10:35 they were warned not to throw away their confidence, which has great *reward.* They are now urged to follow the example of Moses for whom "the reproach of Christ" was of far greater value than all the treasures and pleasures of Egypt. Follow the true Moses, he is saying, the man of uncompromising faith, not the Moses of unbelieving Judaism.

In 13:13 they are encouraged to go forth to Christ outside the camp "bearing the reproach of Him." This is precisely what Moses did. He went forth outside the camp of Egypt, where honour and wealth were his without limit, in order to bear the reproach of Christ. Moses, the founder of their nation, provided the perfect role-model for his wavering kinsmen. Ill-treatment with the people of God, even in the case of Moses, is reckoned by God as bearing the reproach of Christ, on the grounds that Christ is Himself resident in His people and identifies with them (Matthew 25:40; Acts 9:5).

By faith he left Egypt

"By faith he left Egypt, not fearing the anger of the king" (27). This is understood by many as a reference to the Exodus on the grounds that Moses *did* fear the fury of Pharaoh when he left Egypt the first time (Exodus 2:14). But the wording is not appropriate to the Exodus and its position before the Passover (28) points to an earlier occasion.

Moses was indeed afraid when he discovered that "the thing was known", but it does not say that he was afraid of Pharaoh's anger. On the contrary, he was fully prepared to champion his people's cause in the face of Pharaoh's anger. He supposed that his brethren would understand that God would give them deliverance by his hand -- but they understood not (Acts 7:25). It was being rejected by his own people which rendered his mission impossible, and it was by faith (in response to God's express command) that he left Egypt.

He endured as seeing the One unseen. Of all "the things not seen" God is the most important. Those who have genuine faith in the unseen God have no trouble in believing all the other unseen things revealed in His word.

By faith he has kept the Passover

Here we have the third occurrence of the perfect tense in this chapter. It is not "By faith he kept ...", but "By faith *he has kept* (or instituted) the Passover." He observed it that Passover night in Egypt, and it was still being observed when this epistle was written. Like Abraham's offering up Isaac, it was not a single event but a perennial reminder of what the Lord had done and was going to do.

The Passover was kept, not by the blood *sprinkled*, but by the blood daubed and smeared on the doorposts and lintels. A different word is translated "sprinkle" elsewhere in the epistle, and the message is different also from e.g. "the blood of sprinkling that speaks a better word than the blood of Abel" (12:24).

Those commended for their faith
The Red Sea, Jericho and Rahab
Hebrews 11:29-40

"By faith the people crossed the Red Sea as if on dry land." The Israelite people are here credited with faith though from Exodus 14 it would appear that Moses was the only person to exercise true faith. The people accused Moses of cynically planning their extermination in the wilderness! (14:11-12).

Moses courageously replied, "Fear not, stand firm, and see the salvation of the Lord, which he will work for you today..." Moses did not know *how* the Lord would save them, but he had no doubt that He would.

As is usually the case, it was those who complained who made the most noise. There were many others, we may be sure, who *did* have faith that the Lord would save them. According to Exodus 14:10 "the people of Israel cried out *to the Lord*", exactly what Moses was doing himself (15). Once the sea had been divided, they all had faith to cross over.

The walls of Jericho

No city wall has ever collapsed simply by marching round it

thirteen times! Yet the Israelites were prepared to make fools of themselves in obedience to the Lord's command. For the first time in their history the people really were trusting the Lord, under the leadership of Joshua who told them what the Lord was saying. On this occasion the Israelites heard from Joshua (Joshua 6:6-7) what Joshua had heard from the Lord (2-5).

They were beginning to understand the important lesson that "the weapons of our warfare are not carnal, but mighty through God to the pulling down of strongholds" (2 Corinthians 10:4).

By faith Rahab

The harlot Rahab was the only one to have faith in Jericho. They all knew the facts: how the Lord had dried up the water of the Red Sea and what He had done to Sihon and Og, the two kings of the Amorites. They had all felt their hearts melt and their spirits flag, but only Rahab had the faith to believe. "I know that the Lord has given you the land", she said, "... For we have heard how the Lord dried up the water of the Red Sea ... and what you did to the two kings of the Amorites ... the Lord your God, he is God in the heavens above and on earth beneath" (Joshua 2:9-11).

The scarlet line or cord which Rahab placed in the window is in Hebrew *tiqvah*, from a root meaning to stretch out. In every other place where this word occurs (31 times) it is translated *hope* or *expectation*. This cord was Rahab's hope-line, the grounds for her faith in the one thing she hoped for, her rescue from the city doomed to destruction. It was also her life-line; it speaks of the blood of Christ, the same as the blood daubed on the doorposts and lintels which protected the Israelite homes from the ravages of the avenging angel.

She looked for temporal salvation but the Lord gave her eternal salvation through the shed blood of Christ. She married Salmon, the father of Boaz who married Ruth (Matthew 1:5), and her faith is here immortalised along with Abraham, Moses and all the rest. Though a Gentile and a prostitute she obtained by faith a place of honour in the Israel of God. But all her friends and relations who were citizens of Jericho, men and women, young and old, were devoted to destruction along with the city. Another clear warning to the readers of this epistle.

Something better

Time would fail us to tell of Gideon, Barak, Samson and the rest, though the same principle of faith-obedience applied to all of them as well. Through their faith in God's revelation they were given strength to perform incredible feats of heroism and endurance.

In addition to their faith they had all one thing in common: they did not receive what was promised (11:39). God had foreseen something better for believers in Christ that apart from them they should not be made perfect (40). There was at that time, while the Acts period was still in progress, a solidarity and continuity of Old and New Testament believers, united in heritage as well as hope. There could be no perfection for either company before the second coming of Christ, but when that occurred both would be perfected together and would receive their promised reward.

But of course the church of today is altogether different from that represented by Abraham and the recipients of this epistle. It is the body of Christ, a new creation, a new humanity whose hope and position are located in the heavenly places, not (we believe) in the New Jerusalem at all.

Let us lay aside every weight
Hebrews 12

Hebrews 12 begins with the words *Therefore we also* ... Faced with such a formidable cloud of witnesses, it is now our turn to put aside every weight and the sin which clings so closely and to run with endurance the race which lies ahead of us.

The Christian life is regularly compared to running a race. Like an athlete we should exercise self-control and run as if to win the race (1 Corinthians 9:24-27). Paul's overriding aim in life was to finish the course (Acts 20:24), and this he achieved with flying colours (2 Timothy 4:7). I have fought the good fight, he says, using the same word, *agona*, as in Hebrews 12:1.

Jesus the pioneer

Jesus is of course the great exemplar. He is both the author and the finisher of the faith, both the One who strides out in front and finishes first of all. He endured the cross, despising the shame, and is now seated (perfect tense) at the right hand of the throne of God as both victor and king.

This is the only mention of the cross in Hebrews (apart from 6:6). Surprisingly there is no mention of the cross in Romans either except in 6:6 ("this knowing that our old man was crucified with him"). The cross speaks of suffering and the putting to death of the sinful nature. It speaks also of shame. Jesus said, "he who does not take up his cross and follow me is not worthy of me. He who finds his life will lose it, and he who loses his life for my sake will find it" (Matthew 10:38-39). "If we have died with him, we shall also live with him." Yes, but if we would reign with Him, we must learn to endure with Him as well (2 Timothy 2:11-12).

Discipline

The Lord disciplines the one whom He loves and chastises every son whom He receives (6). The writer quotes from Proverbs 3:11-12. According to Deuteronomy 8:5, "as a man disciplines his son, so the Lord your God disciplines you." That is the point: it is *sons* whom the Lord disciplines, so if you feel chastened or chastised it is proof that the Lord is treating you as a son.

To the Laodiceans the Lord says, "Those whom I love, I reprove and discipline, so be zealous and repent" (Revelation 3:19). Indeed, "Blessed is the man whom you discipline, O Lord!" (Psalm 94:12). Of course, all discipline is painful while it lasts, but if at the end it produces "the peaceful fruit of righteousness", it will have been well worth the pain and sorrow.

The advice which springs from this is "*Straighten* the drooping hands and paralysed knees, and *make straight* paths for your feet" (12-13). Strive for peace with all men, holiness without which no-one will see the Lord, and the grace of God which it is possible to miss.

The root of bitterness

So long as one strives after these things there is little chance of the "root of bitterness" springing up (15). This expression looks back to Deuteronomy 29:18-19 where "a root bearing poisonous and bitter fruit" describes the person who, "when he hears the words of this sworn covenant, blesses himself in his heart, saying, 'I shall be safe though I walk in the stubbornness of my heart."

Such a person was Esau who sold his birthright for a single meal. He did so deliberately, confirming it with an oath (Genesis 25:31-33). Later, when he wanted to inherit the blessing, he was rejected for he found no place to repent, though he sought it with tears (27:34, 38). Esau was unable to reverse the decision he had made, and in like manner, "it is impossible to restore again to repentance those who have once been enlightened ... if they fall away..." (Hebrews 6:4-6).

You have come to

First, what they have *not* come to. They have not come to Mount Sinai (18), to a blazing fire, darkness, gloom and tempest, and to a voice so terrible that the hearers begged that no further message be spoken to them. They *have* come to Mount Zion, the city of the living God, the heavenly Jerusalem (22).

Seven things are listed to which they have come near: the heavenly Jerusalem, innumerable angels in festal gathering, the assembly of the firstborn enrolled in heaven, to a Judge who is God of all men, the spirits of just men made perfect, Jesus the mediator of the new covenant, and the sprinkled blood which speaks better things than the blood of Abel.

Most of these look to the future when Christ returns in glory accompanied by the angels to judge His people (Matthew 25:31; Zechariah 14:5). No saint of either covenant has yet been made perfect (Hebrews11:40). As Lang remarks, "the just are not yet made perfect, nor can be till resurrection." The New Jerusalem is the city *which is yet to come* (13:14). Not till Christ returns will "the church of the Firstborn" be unrolled in heaven with every name in place. They may have come to these things, but their realisation is still future.

God is a consuming fire

With these ominous words the chapter concludes. See Deuteronomy 4:24. When God spoke from Sinai "his voice shook the earth", but the time is coming when He will shake the heavens as well. See Haggai 2:6-7; Revelation 6:12-14. Everything will then be removed except the one thing that cannot be shaken, namely the kingdom which the saints will receive. Let us therefore serve Him well-pleasingly with reverence and awe.

Concluding advice
Hebrews 13

"Let brotherly love continue" (13:1). In all the epistles we are exhorted to love one another (e.g. 1 John 3:16-18). This above all is the mark of the Christian. One aspect of love is hospitality. Great emphasis is laid on this since the Christian traveller needed somewhere to stay in a hostile world. Paul always lodged with believers wherever possible (e.g. Acts 18:1-2; Philemon 22). Those in prison or being persecuted for their faith were another cause for concern. They were in urgent need of help and encouragement and the necessities of life provided by loving hands.

More advice follows. "Let marriage be held in honour ... Keep your life free from the love of money." We have a God who has promised never to forsake us, an ever-present helper and provider. We should always be *content*, content with what we have, be it little or much. Paul said he had learnt to be content in whatever situation he found himself (Philippians 4:11-13). If we have food and clothing, with these we should be content. But those who desire to be rich are tempted with many senseless and harmful desires (1Timothy 6:8-10).

Their leaders

Three times in this chapter he mentions their leaders. In v. 7, "Remember your leaders"; v. 17, "Obey your leaders"; v. 24, "Greet all your leaders." In v. 7 he is thinking primarily of past leaders, those who brought them the word of God. "Imitate their faith", he says. Here were a group of witnesses, much closer than those acclaimed in chapter 11, men they had known personally and from whose ministry they had profited. As for their present leaders, they should submit to them, and give them cause for joy by their willing cooperation and obedience.

Don't be led away

They are not to be led astray by strange teachings of various kinds (9). He has in mind the superseded doctrines of Judaism which still exerted an unhealthy pull on these Hebrew believers. He mentions in particular "foods", mentioned also in 9:10, along with drinks and ablutions, as "regulations for the body imposed until the time of reformation."

We have no further use for such foods, for "we have an altar from which those who serve the tent (tabernacle or temple) have no right to eat" (10). Our altar is the sacrifice of Christ from which we derive an imperishable and more satisfying fare, one which endures to eternal life (John 6:27,58).

Outside the camp

On the Day of Atonement, which is here in mind (11), the bull and goat, whose blood was brought into the most holy place to make atonement, were carried outside the camp to be burnt. These animals were not actually slaughtered outside the camp, like the red heifer in Numbers 19, but they were consumed outside the camp (Leviticus 16:27). Outside the camp was a place of ostracism and shame. There the leper was banished for the duration of his illness (Leviticus 13:46), and their offenders were stoned to death, such as the blasphemer (Leviticus 24:14) and the Sabbath-breaker (Numbers 15:35-36).

Jesus also suffered outside the gate in order to sanctify the people through His own blood (12). We too are expected to "go forth to him outside the camp bearing his reproach" (13). This will mean living as strangers and exiles on the earth, like the patriarchs of old, for in this world "we have no lasting city" (14).

We too have sacrifices to offer to God, the sacrifices of praise, doing good, and sharing with others, for such sacrifices are well-pleasing to God (16). We recall that "without faith it is impossible to be well-pleasing to Him" (11:6), and that Enoch, after walking with God for 300 years, "obtained witness to have been well-pleasing to God" (11:5).

Benediction

"Now may the God of peace who brought again from the dead our Lord Jesus, the great shepherd of the sheep, by the blood of the eternal covenant, equip you with everything good that you may do his will, working is us that which is well-pleasing in his sight, through Jesus Christ, to whom be glory for ever and ever. Amen."

The words "shepherd of the sheep" seem to be derived from Isaiah 63:11 (LXX) where, speaking of Moses, it says "Where is he that brought up from the sea the shepherd of the sheep?" The Israelites were led through the Red Sea by the hand of Moses and Aaron who went in front their flock like true eastern shepherds (Psalm 77:20). In the same way our Lord Jesus, the great Shepherd of the sheep, was brought again from the dead at the head of His flock. In due course the flock will follow His lead in orderly ranks (1 Corinthians 15:23). There can be no doubt about that. To Him be the glory for ever and ever!

More on Hebrews

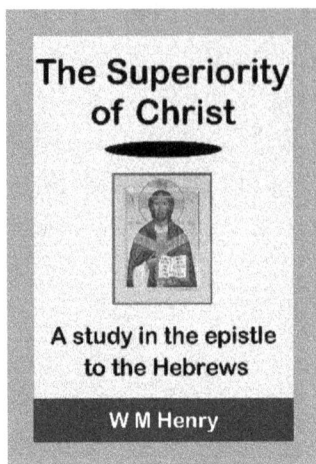

The Superiority of Christ

A study in the epistle to the Hebrews

W M Henry

The purpose of the epistle to the Hebrews is clear; it is to show the superiority of the Lord Jesus Christ to the religious system established by Moses. This is startling in its implications, because Israel's system of worship, and all the rites and rituals that went along with it, were based not on any ideas that Moses had, but on God's revelation to him. What the epistle to the Hebrews reveals is:

- Christ's superiority to the prophets
- Christ's superiority to angels
- Christ's superiority to Moses
- Christ's superiority to Joshua
- Christ's superiority to Aaron
- Christ as the guarantee of a superior covenant
- Christ as the provider of a superior sacrifice

The Superiority of Christ by W M Henry
Published by The Open Bible Trust
www.obt.org.uk

More on the New Covenant

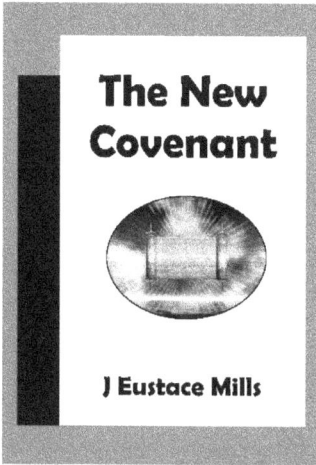

The New Covenant

J Eustace Mills

THE COVENANTS

Ernest Streets

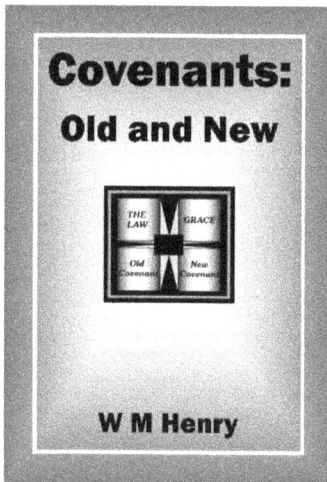

Covenants:
Old and New

THE LAW — GRACE
Old Covenant — New Covenant

W M Henry

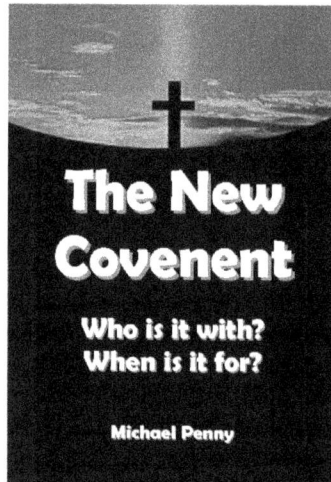

The New Covenent

Who is it with?
When is it for?

Michael Penny

Please visit **www.obt.org.uk** for further details of these books.

These books can be ordered from that website.

They are also available as eBooks from Amazon and Apple and as KDP paperbacks from Amazon..

About the author

Charles Ozanne was born in Crowborough, Sussex, in 1936. He read Theology at Oxford before undertaking research in the book of Revelation for his PhD at the University of Manchester under F. F. Bruce. Some of his recent publications for the Open Bible Trust have been a commentary on Daniel, entitled *Empires of the End-Time;* a critique of Replacement Theology entitled *God's Plan for Israel: Replacement or Restoration?* and a work looking at *The Sabbath and Circumcision.*

One of his latest works is *Understanding the New Testament,* (see next page), which is also available as an eBook. This is a well-written and well-presented commentary on the whole of the New Testament, showing that each of the 27 documents, although distinctive, fit into an overall pattern. For further details of this latest book, and his many others, please visit …

www.obt.org.uk

Also by Charles Ozanne

Understanding The New Testament

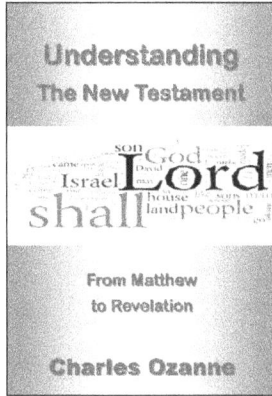

This book is written from the point of view that the New Testament is a single book made up of twenty-seven inter-related parts. Therefore, understanding something of the whole will increase our appreciation of the individual writings.

The author's desire is to give the reader *understanding*, i.e. an understanding of what the whole of the New Testament is about. With that aim in view, he gives us a guided tour through the New Testament, briefly explaining the purpose of each book in turn before giving a synopsis of its teaching.

In this way by examining the parts, the meaning of the whole becomes clearer and ... the meaning of the parts is brought more sharply into focus by understanding the whole.

More details of this book, and the ones on the next page, can be seen on **www.obt.org.uk** from where they can be ordered.

Further details of the books mentioned on these pages can be seen on

www.obt.org.uk

They can be ordered from that website and from

The Open Bible trust
Fordland Mount, Upper Basildon, Reading, RG8 8LU, UK.

They are also available as eBooks from Amazon and Apple and as KDP paperbacks from Amazon.

There are over 30 books written by Charles Ozanne published by The Open Bible Trust. The following is a selection.

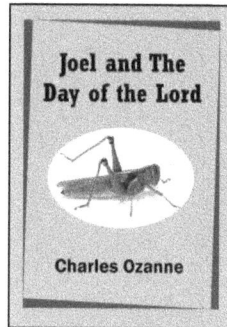

Israel's Appointed Festivals
Charles Ozanne

Sensational Truth In Ephesians
Charles Ozanne

The Fourth Gentile Kingdom
In Daniel & Revelation
Charles Ozanne

God's Plan for Israel
Replacement or Restoration?
Charles Ozanne

Baptism
- rite & reality -
Charles Ozanne

Joel and The Day of the Lord
Charles Ozanne

For more information on these and other publications by Charles Ozanne please visit:

www.obt.org.uk/charles-ozanne

Search Magazine

Charles Ozanne is a regular contributor to *Search magazine.*

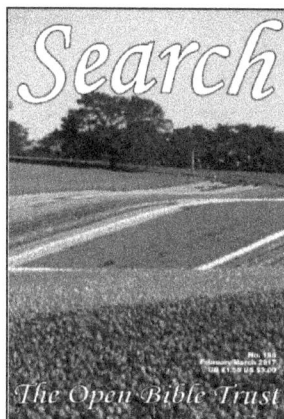

About this book

Introducing Hebrews

The Epistle to the Hebrews has always been of special interest to students of the Bible.

Its individual approach, its Old Testament flavour, its interest in typology are features of particular interest. But most important of all is its emphasis on 'maturity', the need to persevere in patience and faith, and the ever-present danger of backsliding and lapsing into denial of the faith.

We would be unwise to imagine that we are too 'mature' to fall into this danger. So, if we are honest, we shall see ourselves mirrored in this epistle, either as one who is going on to perfection or as one whose faith has grown cold.

Publications of The Open Bible Trust must be in accordance with its evangelical, fundamental and dispensational basis. However, beyond this minimum, writers are free to express whatever beliefs they may have as their own understanding, provided that the aim in so doing is to further the object of The Open Bible Trust. A copy of the doctrinal basis is available on **www.obt.org.uk** or from:

THE OPEN BIBLE TRUST
Fordland Mount, Upper Basildon,
Reading, RG8 8LU, UK

www.ingramcontent.com/pod-product-compliance
Lightning Source LLC
Chambersburg PA
CBHW070531030426
42337CB00016B/2179